BFI TV Classics

BFI TV Classics is a series of books celebrating key individual television programmes and series. Television scholars, critics and novelists provide critical readings underpinned with careful research, alongside a personal response to the programme and a case for its 'classic' status.

Also Published:

Buffy the Vampire Slayer
Anne Billson

Doctor Who
Kim Newman

The Office
Ben Walters

Our Friends in the North
Michael Eaton

Queer as Folk
Glyn Davis

Seinfeld
Nicholas Mirzoeff

The Singing Detective
Glen Creeber

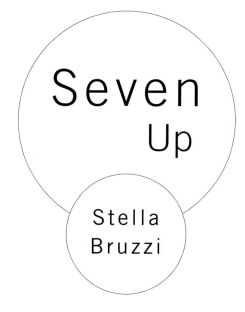

Seven
Up

Stella
Bruzzi

First published in 2007 by the
British Film Institute
21 Stephen Street, London W1T 1LN

The British Film Institute's purpose is to champion moving image culture in all its richness and diversity across the UK, for the benefiit of as wide an audience as possible, and to create and encourage debate.

Images from *Seven Up*, Granada Television.
Page 32 – *The Fishing Party*, BBC TV; p. 39 – *Big Brother* (2000), Bazal Productions.

British Library Cataloguing-in-Publication Data
A catalogue record for this book is available from the British Library

ISBN 978–1–84457–196–3

Set by Fakenham Photosetting Limited, Fakenham, Norfolk
Printed in the UK by The Cromwell Press, Trowbridge, Wiltshire

Contents

v

Acknowledgments

At the BFI I would like to give warmest thanks to my editor Rebecca Barden, Sarah Watt, who took over her job while Rebecca was on maternity leave, Sophia Contento and Tom Cabot. I am also indebted to Brian Winston, who filled me in on the early days of *World in Action*, and to Peter Goddard, who, among other things, let me see the manuscript of his yet unpublished book on the same series. I would like also to thank John Ellis for loaning me his copy of *The Family*, Rachel Moseley and Helen Wheatley. Most of all, though, I would like to extend my deepest gratitude to the director of *Seven Up*, Michael Apted, the series' producer Claire Lewis and two of the 'children', Bruce Balden and Nick Hitchon. The interviews they granted me have proved truly invaluable and this book is infinitely richer for them.

Introduction

Seven Up is the longest-running documentary series on television; having started out as a one-off *World in Action* Special in 1964 about a group of British seven-year-olds it is still being made. Seven years after the first documentary, Michael Apted, one of the two researchers on the original programme, returned to make *7 Plus Seven*, and has returned every seven years since then to interview the 'children' again. The last film to date has been *49 Up*, in 2005. Apted says about *Seven Up* that 'what's great about it is that it dramatises political history' (Apted, 2007), and this study endeavours to look at different aspects of that history. Chapter 1 details the series' production history, Chapter 2 contextualises *Seven Up* within the history of British television documentary and Chapter 3 offers a textual analysis of it. The journey from *World in Action* to *49 Up* has been a monumental one and *Seven Up* has required a considerable amount of personal investment on the part of the film-makers, most significantly perhaps from Apted, whose first job it was and for whom, in his own words, it has become 'the biggest part of any legacy I have' (ibid.), but also for its producer since *28 Up*, Claire Lewis, and the cameraman since *21 Up*, George Jesse Turner. Most of all, however, the personal investment has been on the part of the 'children', the majority of whom still agree to be interviewed when seven years comes around. Apted comments on their continued commitment to the project: 'To have your life up for judgment to a huge audience every seven years, that can't be easy' (ibid.).

The enduring importance of the series can partially be gauged by public responses to it. *Seven Up* has had a greater cultural impact than its viewing figures might suggest; there is, for example, a flurry of press interest around each instalment and as Apted remarks about its unexpected popularity in America: 'It ain't James Bond, but nevertheless it gets an enormous amount of column inches' (ibid.).[1] It is interesting to me, however, that these 'column inches' do not necessarily reflect what I would have predicted they would reflect, namely that, from the very start, the series was obviously going to be considered seminal television. As the series has grown, so popular responses have gained momentum and over time its cultural influence has been affirmed. Although, for example, Granada's press release for *7 Plus Seven* stated that 'critics marvelled' at the original programme and that 'education authorities wanted to borrow the film to show to trainee teachers' (Granada Television, 1970: 1), Nancy Banks Smith in the *Guardian* found *7 Plus Seven* to be less 'effective' than its predecessor, 'difficult to follow' because of the need to 'synchronise two sets of faces'. She concluded: 'I doubt if too much can be deduced from the programme' (Banks Smith, 1970). Banks Smith reviews *Twenty-One* (subsequently *21 Up*) seven years later and still misses the 'sparkling children of "Seven Up!"' who she finds still 'hijacked the show' and had, to her disappointment, 'all grown into respectable, even humdrum, adults' (Banks Smith, 1977). Not even by its third instalment had *Seven Up* become universally acknowledged as a 'television classic': the *New Statesman* also found the two-hour *Twenty-One* dull, closing its short review with the damning observation that 'it soon became embarrassing to see the interviewers trying to drain some sociological usefulness from the random flood of anecdotage on offer' (Hamilton, 1977). These responses, however, contrast with the more positive review of the same episode in the *Daily Telegraph* by Sean Day-Lewis.

It was after the transmission of *28 Up* that the series became iconic; the press responses to this film were both more numerous and, in tenor, slightly different; most significantly, the press's engagement was far more with the individual 'children' as opposed to the attitudes and style of the series as a whole. It is probably not a coincidence that, at *28 Up,* as discussed in Chapter 1, the way in which the films were edited started to change, from interviews being intercut with each other (as they were up to and including *21 Up*) to being cut separately, as they have been hitherto. *28 Up* was also the first programme in the series to be shown in the US, where it became an instant hit at festivals. Andrew Sarris's review for *Village Voice* is indicative of American enthusiasm for the series, saying of *28 Up*: 'The results are both staggering and chastening on so many levels that the entire enterprise may require years of amplification and analysis before we can even begin to answer all the perplexing questions it raises' (Sarris, 1985: 51).

In the UK, Valerie Grove for the *Evening Standard* gushed, 'It was television as a magic mirror, a crystal ball in reverse, able to show people their previous forgotten selves, undistorted by tricks of memory' (Grove, 1984: 25). The most cogent and intelligent review in response to *28 Up* is by Julian Barnes in *The Observer*, who, while liking the series and the children, is perceptive on its limitations and constraints. Barnes speculates, for example, that the intervention of television on these 'ordinary' lives is crucial, that maybe the interviewees, 'conscious down the years of the septennial visits of the TV crew, therefore exerted themselves more than they otherwise would have done' and that the original children were probably selected because they were 'good on television' not because they offered 'a typical cross-section of British society' (Barnes, 1984). The discernment and contrivance of the documentary subject is now, in the era of reality television, a major and continuing concern. An important part of *Seven Up*'s enduring success is that it has never become so anachronistic as to lose its relevance and interest for the modern viewer.

Maybe the underlying reason for *28 Up* being the first time the press (and by extension the public) became attached to the series was that this was the stage at which – with the distance between adult and childhood selves becoming so marked and obvious – the enduring value of the series emerged. It is also in the aftermath of the release of *28 Up* that the public's attachment to the 'children' as detachable elements

3

from the series emerges forcefully. After *35 Up*, the *Daily Mail* ran an article about Sue as a person more than as a television entity. The tone of the piece bears significant similarities to the numerous articles now in magazines such as *Heat* about television-made celebrities; Sue is said to have 'shed both her husband and a stone and a half in weight' between 28 and 35, and in so doing 'appears to have found herself' (Davies, 1991: 13), a perception that the interview with Sue goes on to confirm. This article is illustrative of another pervasive attitude to the series, namely that its audiences seem to respond more positively to the contributors to *Seven Up* the more they get to know them; the series is also a 'classic' because an affinity has been established between the 'children' and the viewers.

The *Seven Up* 'child' who has attracted the most independent press interest has been Neil. Robert Low in *The Observer*, for instance, writes that Neil Hughes has been offered a university place, a job and accommodation by concerned viewers (Low, 1984: 3). It is ironic, though, that the focus on Neil (like the *Daily Mail*'s interest in Sue) became more pronounced in the press at *42 Up*, when Neil was happier and more settled, various articles echoing Matthew Bond's opening remark in his review for the *Daily Telegraph*: 'So we needn't have worried about Neil after all' (Bond, 1998: 40). Although a couple of journalists broke ranks, there was an informal understanding among the majority that the happy ending to Neil's hitherto troubled story should remain secret in advance of transmission. As Peter Paphides writes in *Time Out*, in his preview to *42 Up*: 'we'll have to wait till the very end to discover the bizarre turns that Neil's life continues to take. Such is the allure of his story, that we've been sworn to secrecy' (Paphides, 1998: 26).

What transpires is that *Seven Up*'s longevity is the single most important factor in its emergence as a 'television classic'; that an increased function of it having been around so long is that it has become over time the memorable social document it strove to be instantaneously at the outset. The underlying reasons for the series' appeal are multiple: that it celebrates ordinary lives; that it offers insights not only into the present each time it comes around but into a past that its 'children' share with many of its viewers; that viewers might become fixated on the series as a 'social document'; but perhaps more enduring and personally significant is that they are drawn to the people interviewed for it – possibly as individuals they identify with, but more than likely as individuals they have come to know and/or like.

One point of information: I have referred to the series as *Seven Up*. The series is sometimes known as 'The *Up* Series', but this seemed so clunky and not how anyone I have spoken to about the series refers to it. When I am referring specifically to Paul Almond's 1964 film, I refer to it as 'Seven Up!' – that is, not in italics with the original exclamation mark and within quote marks.

1 Production History

'Seven Up!' was originally intended as a one-off 'Special' for Granada's current affairs strand *World in Action*. Unlike later derivative series such as the BBC's *Seven Up 2000* or *Child of our Time*, the retrospective decision to create a series out of the original Granada film carries both formal and aesthetic implications. Granada Television launched *World in Action* on 7 January 1963 with a report on the nuclear arms race. The series continued until 1998. The first series editor was Tim Hewat, an Australian who had joined Granada in 1957 at the age of twenty-nine, having been Northern Editor on the *Daily Express*. He had been recruited by Denis Foreman, informally Granada's head of programmes, alongside other young journalists such as Bill Grundy, Derek Granger, David Plowright and Jeremy Isaacs and, prior to *World in Action*, had created and produced the current affairs series *Searchlight*, characterised by its 'brash, populist approach' (Goddard *et al.*, 2007: 13). The specific importation of tabloid journalism into factual programming was, Michael Apted believes, Hewat's significant contribution:

> It was largely Hewat who reinvented current affairs and documentaries in the early sixties. He put tabloid journalism on television. Up till then it had been very establishment, very *Panorama*, very much the world of the BBC. His output was peppered with urgent and racy subject matter. It was blue-collar television – noisy, vulgar, quick-witted and of the moment (Quoted in Lewis and Davis, 1991: 6).

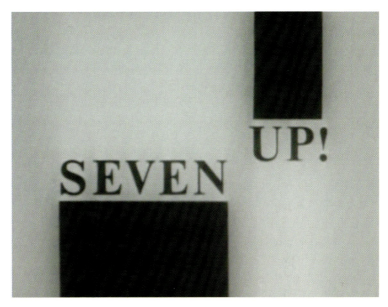

From the title sequence of the original *World in Action*

Like its successor, *Searchlight* was persistently deemed to have breached the 1954 Television Act's requirements of impartiality and, after twenty-seven programmes, was axed. Hewat was not able to establish another similar series for over two years, until the launch of *World in Action*, a series that abandoned the studio and interview format of its current affairs rivals *Panorama* and *This Week* and married a desire to exploit the journalistic potential of the new lightweight 16mm cameras and synchronised sound equipment.[2]

World in Action operated across a range of what could be deemed 'current affairs', from current news stories to stories that reflected more general 'ongoing public concerns' (Goddard *et al.*, 2001: 81). Whereas 'Seven Up!' was more reflective and thesis-driven, *World in Action*'s dramatic reconstruction of the Great Train Robbery was a piece of responsive, immediate current affairs television, transmitted within hours of the trial verdict in January 1963. The urgency of this latter style

of programme was frequently reflected in the films' visual quality, as there
was often no time to produce a clean transmission copy and sometimes
the cutting copy – complete with joins – had to be used (Goddard *et al.*,
2007: 24). 'Seven Up!' exemplified two fundamental aspects of *World in
Action*'s output: its sustained interest in 'the changing face of British
society' (Goddard *et al.*, 2001: 81) and its less frequent production of
films on 'soft' subjects, as Brian Winston, a researcher on the early series
of *World in Action*, terms them, such as profiles of Stanley Matthews or
the Beatles, or a programme about fashion modelling. However, 'Seven
Up!' was by no means a classic *World in Action*; for example, its visual
richness ran entirely counter to what Winston has referred to as Hewat's
'positive anti-aesthetic' (ibid.: 87). Although the series' aesthetics
changed and evolved over time, from the first programme, the *Seven Up*
series has paid considerable attention to aesthetics and style. As Bruce,
one of the original children, has remarked when recounting the time
sound recordist (Nick Steer) and cameraman (George Jesse Turner) took
over a short sequence of him singing in the choir in St Albans abbey for
49 Up, 'they take a great deal of care' (Balden, 2006).

8

Although Hewat remained Executive Producer only until the
end of February 1964 (the other Executive Producer was Derek
Granger), he retained a supervisory role over the series and the original
film bears his imprint, not least because the programme was to a great
extent his idea. As Claire Lewis details:

> Tim Hewat was an Australian ... He saw and was horrified by the rigidity of
> social class in Britain in the 60s and he wanted to make a film about it,
> about how constricting it was and whether or not you could ever escape it.
> His other obsession was the Jesuit 'give me the child' maxim and he put
> those two ideas together. The apocryphal story is that he took two or three
> people to the top of Golden Square [Granada offices]. They looked out over
> London and he said 'I want us to make a film that will find out who will be
> running Britain in the year 2000', which is what it says at the beginning of
> 'Seven Up!' ... It's interesting that it had to be done by someone who wasn't
> British. (Lewis, 2006)

The citation to which Lewis refers here is 'Give me a child until he is seven, and I will give you the man', which was the stated premise for 'Seven Up!' and is attributed to Francis Xavier (1506–1552), the Spanish missionary and co-founder of the Jesuit order.[3] A slightly different version of this story is that Tim Hewat, in conversation with Paul Almond, the director of 'Seven Up!' (a Canadian), came up with the idea of making a programme that probed the British class system by interviewing a sample of children from different social backgrounds. In both versions, however, it becomes clear that the original film presented an outsider's perspective on British society.

Alongside Almond, Hewat and Granger, photography was by David Samuelson and Michael Boultbee, the narrator was Douglas Keay and the programme's two researchers were Michael Apted (in 1963 a Granada graduate trainee for whom 'Seven Up!' was his first job) and Gordon McDougall. Apted and McDougall were responsible for finding what were originally twenty children. Although 'Seven Up!' was granted a six-week research period – roughly five times as much as a weekly *World in Action* had – the children had to be found in only three weeks. Apted recalls:

> I did the London stuff, Gordon found the northern children – Neil, Peter, Nick. I did the East End kids, the three posh boys, I think, I definitely did Bruce and I think I found Suzy. We had very little time to do it so he did the rural ones and I concentrated on the southern ones. (Apted, 2007)

The two researchers had rung round education departments in various boroughs who recommended schools; then, when they arrived at each school, the form teachers would 'recommend the children they thought would be best in front of the camera, and we took it from there' (Apted in Lewis and Davis, 1991: 7). On a few occasions, children from the same class were chosen, a decision that has meant it was always going to be harder to obtain a broad social cross-section. Andrew, John and Charles attended the same preparatory school in Kensington; their counterparts are the three East End girls Jackie, Sue and Lynn, who were

Peter and Neil

Nicholas

Jackie, Lynn and Sue

John, Andrew and Charles

pupils together at an East London state primary; Simon and Paul lived at the same children's home; Tony, the East End boy, was also interviewed for 'Seven Up!' alongside his classmate Michelle. Bruce – at boarding school when 'Seven Up!' was made – remembers that the researchers had originally wanted to use two boys from there, but in the end only interviewed him (Balden, 2006). Finally, the two middle-class representatives, Neil and Peter, were classmates and both from the same comfortable Liverpool suburb. The other children were interviewed singly, but still very much in evidence is a preoccupation with balance, with creating pairings and binary opposites through which the underlying arguments could be explored and illustrated: the three privileged boys are inevitably juxtaposed with – and frequently intercut

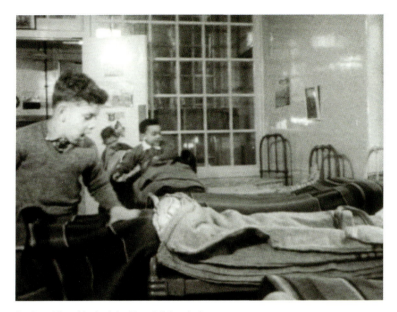

Paul making his bed in the children's home   11

with – the three East End girls; Nick comes to represent the working-class rural community, in contrast to Suzy, from a wealthy rural background; the two 'controls' were Neil and Peter, the ones in the middle; and Bruce feels his counterpoints were Paul and Simon: 'I think they might have been contrasting ... myself with the other two boys in the Barnardo's home because we were all at boarding schools, away from home. I don't know' (ibid.).

   It was then Foreman's idea to make a second film about the children in 'Seven Up!'. As Michael Apted recalls: 'I was sitting in Granada and Denis Foreman came up to me, probably five years after the original programme and said "Why don't we see what happened to those kids? And why don't you do it?" So we went and did it' (Apted, 2007). The result was *7 Plus Seven*, which was transmitted 15 December 1970. By this time, Apted was working in both drama and documentary at Granada, having started his drama career on *Coronation Street* in

1967, where he first worked with writer Jack Rosenthal, with whom he subsequently collaborated on various individual dramas, including 'There's a Hole in Your Dustbin, Delilah' and 'Your Name's Not God It's Edgar' (both 1968) for *Playhouse* and the 1970 series *The Lovers*. Apted remembers that it was easy enough to track down the kids for *7 Plus Seven*, but that there were too many of them, so his first decision was deciding 'which to leave out' (ibid.). The original kids had been selected with only the specific agenda of the first programme in mind, 'Seven Up!' 'wasn't planting any seeds for the future' (ibid.) so Apted narrowed the number of children down from twenty to fourteen by omitting those who duplicated or overlapped with others. The researcher for *7 Plus Seven* was Margaret Bottomley and photography was by Tony Mander. It was still not certain at this stage that this was to become a series; that decision was made after *21 Up*.

Apted continued to direct television drama into the 1970s (other Rosenthal scripts such as 'Another Sunday and Sweet F.A.' in 1972; several BBC *Play for Todays* in 1973 and back to Granada and Thames Television in 1974–5), but in 1972 he directed his first feature film, *The Triple Echo*, with Glenda Jackson and Oliver Reed, which was followed by *Stardust* in 1974 (produced by David Puttnam) and *Squeeze* in 1977. By the time Apted came to make *21 Up* (then credited as *Twenty-One*) for transmission 9 May 1977, he was living in Los Angeles. *21 Up* was produced by the researcher of *7 Plus Seven*, Margaret Bottomley, and was the first in the series to be shot by cameraman George Jesse Turner, who has shot all subsequent episodes. Bottomley died between *21* and *28*, to be replaced as researcher and then producer by Claire Lewis. The degree of continuity through the series has increased and is the primary reason – alongside the obvious factor that *Seven Up* has charted the development into adulthood of several children – for Lewis frequently likening the experience of working on it to being part of a family. The 'team' since *28 Up* has comprised Apted, Lewis (first as researcher, then as producer), George Jesse Turner and Nick Steer (sound recordist): 'But we are now a family … it's now a collaboration and they (the "children") all feel responsible to each other and we all feel responsible to a certain extent' (Lewis, 2006). Every seven years, Lewis maintains,

> is like a family reunion ... We can to go Australia to see Paul or America to see Nick – and we haven't seen him in seven years, although we've emailed, we've phoned – and you walk in and it's like seeing your brother, or your cousin or your auntie. You pick up exactly where you left off as if no time had intervened, and they (the 'children') love it, it's wonderful. (Ibid.)

Lewis assiduously nurtures the *Seven Up* 'family', in part because, when she joined the production team for *28 Up*, she found that nobody in the intervening years had kept tabs on the series' interviewees and as a result one of them in particular – Neil – proved hard to find. As Lewis explains,

> it took me three months to find Neil ... he was completely missing ... by twenty-eight his parents hadn't seen him ... Once I'd found Neil – I had to employ all the methods of a private detective – I had to keep tabs on him, which wasn't very easy. (Ibid.)

13

When she did find him, Neil was in North Wales, about to go to the Highlands of Scotland, which is where he is filmed for *28 Up*. Simon was also hard to trace: 'his mum had died and I had no address for him' (eventually Lewis found him via the electoral register) and the girls 'had all got married and changed their names' (ibid.). Logistically, it is primarily Lewis who holds the 'family' together, although the consistency among the crew and the mutual trust and responsibility it has engendered has no doubt contributed to the series' longevity.

Despite this fervent belief in the family ethos and the relationships that bind personnel and interviewees, not all the 'children' have continued to participate. The first to leave was Charles Furneaux, who ironically works in documentaries (and was, for example, one of the executive producers on Kevin Macdonald's *Touching the Void* [2003]). Apted and Lewis have tried repeatedly to coax Furneaux back, but since *21* he has refused to appear.[4] Prior to *49 Up* he threatened to sue

14   Charles' last interview at twenty-one

Granada on grounds of invasion of privacy and requested that he be cut out of the entire series (which, considering he is interviewed three times alongside John and Andrew, would have rendered much of the footage of the three boys unusable). Granada refused and although Apted has in the past (in part because Furneaux is in the same profession) offered him far more editorial control than he ever has any of the others, he is now resigned to never getting Charles back and has stopped inserting the barbed references to Furneaux that peppered earlier instalments (Apted, 2006). After *28 Up* Peter also left, although Apted has not given up hope entirely of getting him back (ibid.). Peter was singled out by several reviewers after *28* for having 'become a lethargic, disillusioned teacher' (Barnes, 1984) and for being the 'most depressing' of the programme's interviewees, as both the *Evening Standard* and the *Sunday Telegraph* describe him (Grove, 1984: 25; Purser, 1984: 17). Fellow interviewee Nick has mentioned how 'It's tremendously sad that Peter dropped out;

he was one of the most appealing people' (Highton, 2006). A further reason for Peter's departure to the one proffered by Apted is that he was not entirely happy with the image of himself and his then wife Rachel in *28 Up*, commenting about the film-making process that 'The problem we have is when the camera perceives people maybe accurately, but doesn't match people's perceptions of themselves' (Lewis, 2006). Maybe a reason for Nick feeling sympathy for Peter is that he too found the representation of himself and his first wife Jackie in *28 Up* to be harsh.[5] *49 Up* then saw Suzy signing off, having been unhappy throughout with the way she has been portrayed: at seven 'the posh rich girl who didn't like coloured people' (ibid.). John has intermittently refused to take part, staying out of *28 Up* because he did not like the way he had come across in *21* and later not appearing in *42*, and Simon was missing from *35 Up* but back for *42*. Since *35 Up* Lewis and not Apted has conducted the interviews with John, as she did Jackie's for *35 Up* (although, in Lewis's words, 'by *42* Jackie had mellowed a bit' [ibid.] and was again talking to Apted).

Partly as a result of its longevity, the series has had to change formally and adapt to the amount of material that has been accrued over the years. *28 Up* was significant in this respect as the first episode to be structured as a series of vignettes, each individual story being recounted separately, spread over two nights' television. Prior to this the interviews had been intercut, the cross-editing maximising the opportunities to offer a socio-political critique of class, background and the Xavier saying. There are both logistical and more subjective or ideological reasons for this fundamental structural change: that the material was simply becoming too unwieldy to structure in the original, contrapuntal way; that, as Apted has consistently maintained, the series was becoming less political in its emphasis; that the more viewers became engrossed in it, the more the programme-makers realised they were becoming engrossed in the individual stories perhaps more than the underpinning political subtext. *28 Up* was unexpectedly successful in the US, which was a major turning point. The series' politics, however, have not disappeared necessarily as its structure has altered, although they have become implicit, embedded within the personal stories as

15

opposed to more directly imposed. Later episodes are ostensibly less preoccupied with class issues than earlier ones, but social differences and disparities are still present, as Nick argues:

It was all about class when we were little. The class issues with us seven-year-olds were glaringly obvious, and I think it's going to be glaringly obvious in terms of how we age ... so even if they're not talking about class I think it's still evident to anyone who chooses to see it. I don't think people talk about it. As we get older, as you say, there are other issues, one of the most important being 'How dare you, Michael, ask us these questions that make us look so bad?' (Hitchon, 2006)

As Lewis has argued, the 'cross-editing is much nicer in some ways in terms of the film structure' but the material became hard to manage (Lewis, 2006). There have been acknowledgments of the earlier cross-editing style, such as the montage at the end of *42 Up* in which people were asked about the programme, but a return to contrapuntal editing would be impractical. As it is, each episode of *Seven Up* remains roughly the same length as the one before, which normally means that much of the immediately preceding episode is cut each time, as the tendency is to preserve the material that has been selected from the first and second programmes. Time constraints and the truncation of recent history in favour of contemporary history on the one hand and more distant history on the other will be discussed in more detail in relation to Neil in Chapter 3.

Alongside the formal shift at *28 Up*, the greater emphasis upon individuals and personality has also led to a loose running order being established: Tony's, for example, has become the opening vignette since *28* and another persistent narrative feature has been that, from *35 Up*, each instalment has concluded with Neil. Likewise, the two trios (Andrew, John and Charles; Jackie, Lynn and Sue) have traditionally been grouped together, although at *49 Up* the girls' stories are, for the first time, separated out. The overall feel of the interviews has also altered, probably with the switch from 16mm film to digital at *49 Up*, because, as Bruce noticed, the transition 'speeded things up a bit because you didn't have to pause every ten minutes' (Balden, 2006).

Seven Up's longevity has also prompted various international versions. Elsewhere, its structure has been imitated, more or less loosely, by other film-makers wanting to use the idea of revisiting the same people after a gap of several years. In the era of the formatted documentary, it is intriguing that a series as superficially old-fashioned as *Seven Up* could be argued to be a prototype for the dominant trend in factual broadcasting since the millennium, namely the evolution, patenting and international sale of commercially viable programme formats.[6]

Age 7 in America and *Age 7 in the USSR* were started by Granada in 1991; Lewis is the series editor for both series and Apted the producer, or 'consulting producer' as he is credited on *USSR*. *Age 7 in South Africa* started in 1992, again made by Granada, while *7 Up in Germany* and *7 Up in Japan* also began in 1992, and were co-produced by Granada. *America* and *USSR* were begun around the time of *35 Up*, with the express intention of following 'the two great powers over the next fifty years' (Lewis, 2006). However, within a few months of filming *Age 7 in the USSR* the Soviet Union had fallen apart, which, as Lewis puts it, 'was fascinating to us, absolutely fascinating. We just got there in time' (ibid.). The opening voiceover of *Age 7 in the USSR* acknowledges that the film will chart the disintegration of the Soviet Union and that the children, though born in 'the early, optimistic days of *perestroika*' now live in a society that has 'turned to discord'. *Age 7 in the USSR* opens optimistically enough, with the children going off to school for the first time (as they also will be subsequently at the start of the Japanese series), but by the time *Age 14* came around the children were all in different republics.

Socially, the South African series is also notable, because it has charted the post-apartheid era. One might talk about class divisions still being in evidence in the UK *Seven Up*, but the political issues of the South African series are far more extreme. Prior to *21*, for instance, two of the children had died of AIDS (Lewis, 2006) and, as one of the black

17

seven-year-olds remarks: 'we have problems, lots of problems … like killing each other'. *Age 7 in America* looked slightly different from the outset as the co-producers would not countenance the idea of a film without a presenter, so Meryl Streep was brought in to front it. *America* opens with Streep explaining that the *Seven Up* cycle has reached 35, then remarking that the children selected for *America* are 'black, white, yellow … just like the rest of us'. As in the original 'Seven Up!', the children first encounter each other at the zoo, the images accompanied by Streep's voice remarking 'we look at them and we see judgments on today'. The similarities with the UK series' original aims are rather telegraphed here (the three Upper East Side girls are even interviewed sitting together on a sofa, making the parallels with John, Andrew and Charles unmistakable), and *America* appears far stiffer and more regimented than its Soviet or South African counterparts. It seems to have been the American repackaging of *Seven Up* that was the format franchised out to Germany and Japan, both of which are fronted – for international broadcast – by British actress Patricia Hodge rendering very similar introductions in which she explains the *Seven Up* format over images of (in the German version) the children's obligatory visit to the zoo, concluding in both that the 'children speak for themselves'.

There are also documentaries that are more tangentially linked to *Seven Up*, for example, a series of longitudinal films made by women directors that focus exclusively on women. Three such documentaries are Marilyn Gaunt's *Class of '62 – Still Going Strong* (made in 1995 and revisiting women first featured in the earlier film *Class of '62*), Gillian Armstrong's *Not Fourteen Again* (1996) and its three predecessors (*Smokes and Lollies* [1977], *14's Good, 18's Better* [1981], *Bingo, Bridesmaids and Braces* [1988]) and Annie Goldston's *Sheilas: 28 Years On* (2004). Gaunt's films feature women from the same class as Gaunt in Leeds; Armstrong's documentaries are about three working-class girls from Adelaide and how they fare into adulthood; and Goldston's film returns to interview a cross-section of women first interviewed for a documentary series on New Zealand television in the 1970s. None of these was made in direct response to

Seven Up, but all were aware of Apted's series and the comparisons that could be made with it. Directed by and featuring women, these documentaries possess an entirely different relationship to women's history and politics than *Seven Up* could ever do; they are more personal and emotional about women's lives and they all – but particularly Gaunt's moving, evocative films – focus to a far greater extent on the political implications of any woman's relationship with the domestic sphere and how this impacts on her ability to work and achieve independence. *Seven Up*'s lack of women highlights one of the basic problems of the longitudinal documentary project, namely that, having decided to return to film the seven-year-olds again, Apted was also consenting not to tamper with the original selection (bar reducing the number of children). Lewis and Apted later sought to redress the series' gender imbalance by including more of the wives and girlfriends of the male interviewees ('particularly Australian Sue and Tony's Debbie' [Apted 2007]), but it is clear that imitators of *Seven Up* have been more scientific in their approach to selection and more sensitive to potential political imbalances.

19

The BBC have made two series that resemble *Seven Up*: the direct copy *Seven Up 2000*, which is filming again in 2007, and the less directly imitative *Child of Our Time*, which started on 1 January 2000 and filmed a group of parents with babies born around the millennium to whom Robert Winston returns annually. The parents include disabled artist Alison Lapper, a couple who have conceived twins with the help of IVF, another couple who are expecting naturally conceived triplets and who already have three children. While it has caused the film-makers endless problems since 1965, the selection of the children to appear in *Seven Up* seems refreshingly random compared to the rigid, clinical selection of babies for *Child of Our Time*. That this is a scientific as opposed to a socially intriguing or even voyeuristic exercise is signalled through this choice of babies, doubly emphasised by the series being fronted by Winston, one of the pioneers of fertility treatment in the UK. Thus the question of 'seeing if it's genes or environment that makes us what we are' becomes almost as much an issue of health and lifestyle as it does about education and class – although all of these invariably and invaluably intersect. Most recently, Channel 4 have embarked on another imitative series, *Child Genius* (8 February 2007), which will follow a group of gifted children into adulthood, to see 'if they become the 'leaders … of their generation', or fail to fulfil their potential, as many have in the past', as the opening narration attests. Once again, the similarities with the original *Seven Up!* film for *World in Action* are notable, although, like the other copycat series, the 'child geniuses' have been more strategically selected.

This proliferation and diversification of the *Seven Up* prototype is immediately indicative of the production's value and influence. This book is first and foremost a study of *Seven Up* the series; however, its importance within both broadcasting and documentary history will be the basis for the next chapter, which will focus on the interrelationship between *Seven Up* and the evolution, since the early 1960s, of British documentary.

2 The Place of *Seven Up* within British Documentary History

49 Up, to date the last in the series, seemed especially reflexive, the 'children' particularly aware of the act of filming, notions of contrivance and performance. At the end of her interview Suzy, who has always been a reluctant participant, says in response to Apted's question 'Have you had enough of being in the film?': 'Who knows in seven years whether I'll be done again, but this is me saying hopefully I'll reach my half-century and I shall bow out.' The increased reflexiveness of this last instalment has been viewed by Apted and Lewis as a fairly direct testament to the influence of reality television – although Apted states categorically that 'I think that was in their minds, it wasn't in my mind' (Apted, 2007). There is, for example, Jackie's argument with Apted (examined in more detail in Chapter 3) that, on the surface, possessed similarities with 'reality television' and the formatted documentaries that had grown around it. Of this interaction with contemporary factual programming around *49 Up,* Apted speculates that it

> had become an issue in a way it hadn't been before – were we lumped in with a whole scenario of exploitative, cheap, primetime television? I think they're asking themselves 'Is this what we've been part of all these years?' They definitely wanted to talk about it. (Ibid.)

Because of the particular synergies with the dominant culture of factual broadcasting in the early 2000s, how *Seven Up* relates to television documentary in general is currently especially interesting. Modern 'factual entertainment' (such as reality television) specifically signals its constructedness through its very form; it also fails to make a definitive distinction between the 'real' person and the 'performance', a slippage that frequently troubles critics but that nevertheless lies at the heart of Jackie's attack on Apted and her greater willingness to break the code of a series such as *Seven Up*. The series is also, conversely, an intriguing documentary subject because, despite its topicality, it has remained virtually unchanged for over forty-two years and so has proved to be, as a text, stable, resilient and not overly subservient to the shifting tendencies in documentary film-making. In keeping with its longevity and relative stability, *Seven Up* is also representative of a persistent fixation in British cinema and television documentary upon the quotidian and the personal – and how best to show them.

The original programme blended an interest in the ordinary, non-celebrity lives of its children with a significant political agenda. As an Independent Television Authority (ITA) memo from 1964 discussing a number of contentiously political current affairs programmes made by Granada in that year suggests, 'although not edited before transmission' (for impartiality etc.), 'Seven Up!'

> was subsequently seen as primarily designed to illustrate, and indeed emphasise, a social, economic and educational gulf in this country, and to have achieved this end by a careful selection of participants and by subtle editing. It could well have been interpreted as a general argument in favour of State education. (ITA Paper 126 [64])

Notwithstanding the programme's 'soft' origins, it fell firmly within an already established and still vibrant British tradition of small 'p' political documentary and realist film-making. The editing, for example, which the ITA singles out here could be characterised as a 'soft' version of intellectual montage: interested in juxtaposing alternatives (such as class differences, educational differences, ideological differences) but not in order to ram home a strong political message. Instead, as Douglas Keay's voiceover says, the strategy of this original programme is to temper its underpinning, latent didacticism with a less clearly biased, more passive notion of arriving at a conclusion via exploration and observation. For example, the opening line of voiceover is, '*World in Action* enters the struggling, changing world of the seven-year-old,' thereby laying out its observational stall, while, barely a minute later, Keay remarks, 'They're like any other children – except they come from startlingly different backgrounds,' a line that has been repeated in all of the programmes since.

Apted's series is frequently but confusingly likened to films of the Direct Cinema movement (such as Robert Drew's *Primary* [1960]), I assume because they are roughly contemporaneous. However, the series as a whole is far from observational (for a start, it is based upon a series of interviews) and the first film in particular is heavily didactic in style and tone. More than anything *Seven Up* exemplifies the sustained and characteristic fascination in British documentary and the realist dramatic tradition with the life more ordinary, more than with observation *per se*. An important aside to this discussion would be the possible reasons for the relative critical neglect of both Free Cinema and *Seven Up*. The big story of late 1950s'–mid-1960s' documentary is technological advancement – that 16mm became smaller and lighter, that film stock became better able to deal with low light and that synch sound was made possible by the greater portability of new recording equipment. This story is automatically and invariably told within histories of documentary in relation to Direct Cinema, although it could just as interestingly be demonstrated with reference to Free Cinema: from the release of *Every Day Except Christmas* (1957) to that of *We Are the Lambeth Boys* (1959) barely two years later, for instance, one can see the arrival – and dramatic impact – of synch sound. As Karel Reisz remarked, during roundtable discussion chaired by Kevin Macdonald at the National Film Theatre (NFT) on 22 March 2001, John Fletcher, the 'technical wizard' of Free Cinema,

23

welcomed on *The Lambeth Boys* the opportunity to shoot synchronous
sound on unrehearsed material ... we didn't know what was going to
happen, and that was technically extremely advanced for the time, and
Jean Rouch, the great French documentary maker said that these films
of ours started him on all his ethnographic films. (NFT, 2001)

Free Cinema is a relatively neglected branch of the international
observational documentary movement of the late 1950s and early
1960s, probably marginalised in favour of the French cinéma vérité
movement or the American Direct Cinema movement because its main
exponents (Lindsay Anderson, Tony Richardson and Karel Reisz)
swiftly abandoned documentary film-making for feature films. This shift
from non-fiction to fiction in turn gives a pertinent insight into *Seven
Up*, as the social realism of films such as Reisz's *Saturday Night and
Sunday Morning* (1960) or Richardson's *A Taste of Honey* (1961)
suggested other ways in which issues of class and social divisiveness
could be 'softened' through dramatisation without being marginalised.
(There is also an obvious parallel between the Free Cinema directors and
Michael Apted, who likewise made the rapid transition to television
drama and film directing.)

'Free Cinema' was the label given to a brief series of largely
British documentary films screened at the National Film Theatre from
1956–9, specifically, as the programme notes for Season One (5–8
February 1956) state, to differentiate them from more commercial,
industry-funded and thus supposedly compromised feature films. The
Free Cinema manifesto is elusive but evocative of the director's idealism:

No film can be too personal. The image speaks, sound amplifies and
comments. Size is irrelevant. Perfection is not an aim. An attitude means a
style. A style means an attitude. Implicit in our attitude is a belief in freedom,
in the importance of people and in the significance of the everyday.[7]

As with the use of pointed editing in 'Seven Up!', what is being indicated
here is that the Free Cinema directors saw style and choice of subject as

24

attitudes in themselves; that a point could be made simply through giving 'people' and the 'everyday' screen time. Raymond Durgnat, dismisses Free Cinema for achieving only 'a kind of middle-class left-wing sentimentality within the purlieus of the art cinema and the film society' (Durgnat 1970: 128), concluding that the movement offered nothing new at all and was merely 'a highly self-conscious part of an inevitable and massive trend'. He is being harsh, as the concentrated body of work that made up Free Cinema did show how documentary could adopt some of the Lukácsian tropes of drama, for example, by using individuals to represent contrasting, sometimes conflicting social groups. Probably Durgnat is correct to suggest that these are middle-class films that treat those at either extreme of the social spectrum as interesting and freakish, and 'Seven Up!' could be accused of doing much the same. What is significant about the sequence in 'Seven Up!' showing the class of 'posh boys' singing 'Waltzing Matilda' in Latin and

25

The prep-school boys singing 'Waltzing Matilda' in Latin

the sequence in *Momma Don't Allow* (1956) in which the well-to-do jazz enthusiasts arrive at the club and dance awkwardly, self-consciously alongside the free-moving, confident and fluent working-class couples is not that it is stating the obvious – which it is – but that it is using observation to make a 'soft' comment about social difference. *We Are the Lambeth Boys* is the Free Cinema film that 'Seven Up!' echoes most closely: its subjects are teenagers as opposed to children, but the unformed and naive views they spout (their views on capital punishment which, as Durgnat remarks, are 'decidedly at the Alf Garnett end of the spectrum' [ibid.: 127]), as well as the manner in which they are used to evoke and function as the representatives of a recognisable social class, offer parallels with Almond's documentary.

What had also not been possible much earlier had been sustained location filming on feature films. The moment of transition here was *A Taste of Honey*, shot entirely on location in Salford and Blackpool, unlike earlier British New Wave films such as *Saturday Night and Sunday Morning*, another Woodfall production released only a year previously, which had made substantial use of studio sets. The immediacy of Richardson's adaptation of Shelagh Delaney's play is aspired to in 'Seven Up!', which used a hand-held camera in particular to draw its audience into identifying with the children, a feature of the original film's *mise en scène* that is discussed in greater detail in the next chapter. By the mid-1960s the advancements that had been made in cinema – both fiction and documentary – were becoming equally influential in television. Indeed, it could be argued that the British New Wave was as short-lived as Free Cinema had been, as, with the release in 1963 of the big-budget, far more flamboyant *Tom Jones* (Richardson for Woodfall, with a screenplay by John Osborne), the tradition of 'gritty realism' had been passed onto television – both fiction and documentary.[8]

In November 1965 the BBC launched *Man Alive*, its own social subject documentary and current affairs series. Like *World in Action*, *Man Alive* occupied a thirty-minute slot and the series started on 4 November 1965 with 'The Heart Man', a documentary about Texan heart surgeon Michael de Bakey. The second-week slot was filled by 'The Man Who Started the War', a study of Nazi secret agent Alfred Naujocks, who masterminded the German attack on a radio station on the Polish border which transmitted a bogus anti-German broadcast that was used as the catalyst for the German invasion of Poland. Naujocks escaped lightly with only three years' imprisonment, but as the programme is made – using the title of his own memoirs – he fears, particularly in the immediate aftermath of the trial and execution of his old friend Adolf Eichmann, that his past will catch up with him. This, Jeremy James's commentary informs us, is Naujocks's first interview for film; why he agrees to make the programme is never clarified. The format of this *Man Alive* episode suggests how in keeping with the factual output of its time 'Seven Up!' was. James's voiceover, for instance, is extremely dominant and insistent (it really would be impossible to follow 'The Man Who Started the War' without it), much as Douglas Keay's is; it also manifestly tells the *Man Alive* audience how it should respond to the film and how the accompanying images should be interpreted. After orchestrating the successful attack on the radio station Naujocks informed Nazi headquarters and then went to bed; the voiceover says melodramatically: 'Naujocks slept for eight hours and freedom slept for six years,' over archive of Nazi tanks and infantry thundering into Poland. This episode of *Man Alive* has a dramatic story to tell (although the presumed conclusion – Naujocks's capture or final evasion of the Nazi-hunters – is never reached), which is told via an interview with Naujocks (the first) and lengthy sequences of Naujocks, often in close-up, going home or walking through the crowded streets of Hamburg enacting his desired anonymity. One shot stands out: a low-angle close-up of Naujocks's face in a sequence in which the voiceover stresses his loneliness; the purpose of this and the other mute shots of Naujocks's features is, presumably, to make us scrutinise this unpenitent, elegant Nazi. Never does 'The Man Who Started the War' explicitly attack Naujocks's politics, but its point of view is not hidden behind equivocation and balance; the programme-makers, rather like Almond and the *World in Action* team, appear confident in their interpretation of this story and equally sure that in

27

bringing this story to the attention of a television audience they are doing the right thing. As the concluding voiceover remarks: 'He's a man with a past he's not being allowed to forget.'

As its filming style and choice of subjects suggests, *Man Alive* was principally about people and as Harold Williamson, one of the series' early producers, was later to acutely and entertainingly characterise, it was a strand that eschewed 'professional talkers, or politicians, or academics, or self-styled experts' in favour of 'those who'd lived the experience' and whose

> stories, vividly expressed in their own words, reflected almost every facet of social significance that had grabbed public attention over the past ten to 15 years: abortion, mugging, gays, swinging Sixties, drug-taking, body-building, arson, contraception, women in prison, senility, health foods, alternative medicine, neighbours, whiz kids, worker sit-ins, torture, children in care ... (Williamson, 1983: 8)

28

With the arrival of drama series such as the BBC's *The Wednesday Play* (30 September 1964–20 May 1970), which in its first two years broadcast Ken Loach's *Up the Junction* (3 November 1965) and *Cathy Come Home* (16 November 1966), the recounting of topical subjects via individual stories defined much drama as well as documentary output in the mid- to late 1960s. Although this is discernibly the dominant trend of the time in both documentary and realist drama, it would be entirely erroneous to suggest that this approach was the only one. In 1967, for example, the BBC launched its long-running arts programme *Omnibus* (13 October 1967) – using a similar format to its science counterpart *Horizon*, which had begun in May 1964 – and in 1969 the hugely influential *Civilisation* was shown, Kenneth Clark's landmark series examining the ideas and values that to him give meaning to the term 'Western civilisation'.

The second instalment in the *Seven Up* series – *7 Plus Seven* – was transmitted 15 December 1970. In terms of British television documentary history, the 1970s were years of consolidation as well as innovation, with the continuation of the major series from the 1960s. The 'lecture' format continued with Jacob Bronowski's series *The Ascent of Man* (1973), while *Horizon* and *Omnibus* were joined in 1977 by the BBC's religious affairs strand *Everyman*. The format of these latter three is significant and consistent: they are didactic programmes about a single historical or contemporary issue that fall into a shared general subject area (science, the arts, spirituality); they have frequently but by no means exclusively been presenter-led; they are often celebratory. The inherent didacticism of these strands is echoed in a series such as Thames Television's monumental *The World at War* (1974–5), which in turn has influenced just about every historical series since – particularly those whose focus is again World War II. At the opposite end of the documentary spectrum are observational series such as Paul Watson's *The Family* (BBC, 1974), a British version of Craig Gilbert's *The American Family* (1973). Watson's series began transmission before shooting was over and became 'a documentary about an "average" family whose private life is repeatedly exposed on national television' (Winston, 1995: 205), well before – but certainly paving the way for – docusoaps in the latter 1990s.

29

In much of her work artist Gillian Wearing has interrogated the representations of reality found in British television documentaries such as *The Family* and *Seven Up*, which she often cites as a particularly important influence on her work (Tate, 2001; Schwabsky, 2004). Of her 2006 work 'Family History', a work centred on her memories of watching *The Family* as a child, Wearing remarks: 'I found it surprising watching normality … There had been nothing like it on British television. There was *Coronation Street*, but that was too acted, too nostalgic to be real' (Jeffries, 2006). *Seven Up* is arguably compelling for comparable reasons: it is surprisingly interesting watching other people talk about their ordinary lives. As Sue remarks at the end of *42 Up*:

> Before the film starts you think, 'What on earth have I done in that last seven years that I could possibly talk about?'. Then you panic and think

'I should have done something dramatic' … I was hoping I'd win the lottery last night, but life's not like that.

There is an intense and arguably voyeuristic interest in banality at the heart of both a series such as *The Family* and, although executed quite differently, *Seven Up*. There is also a shared interest in the intermingling of intrusion with observation and Paul Watson's work since *The Family*, such as *The Fishing Party* (1986) and *Sylvania Waters* (1993), reinvigorated this documentary tradition.

    Considering the intrusiveness of *Seven Up*, there is an affecting moment in *49 Up* when Tony's wife Debbie reflects upon Tony's admission on camera during his interview for *42 Up* that he had been unfaithful to her, commenting, 'I wish things that were said then were never said', before recounting that their daughter Perry had not gone to school for three weeks after the programme had gone out because of the shock the revelation caused. As Debbie muses: 'you are their mum and dad'. As with either *The Family* or *Man Alive*, what *Seven Up* is perpetually doing is 'coaxing' its subjects (as Williamson suggests) into making personal revelations for the benefit and entertainment of camera and audience. Williamson is recalling his experiences of revisiting subjects of early episodes of *Man Alive* for a new series *Only Time Would Tell* (1983). He recounts his attempts to track these people down and the discovery that many of them did not want to appear in any follow-up programme or be reminded of their past. Williamson discovered that, although in many cases, the filming experiences had been happy ones, the problem had been the aftermath: that

> For a long time after the programme went out – sometimes for years afterwards – they had been got at by neighbours, or family, or colleagues who, for one reason or another, were angered, outraged, ashamed, envious or offended by their television broadcast. (Williamson, 1983: 8)

The peculiar brand of notoriety that follows an appearance in an intrusive observational programme such as *Man Alive*, *The Family* or arguably *Seven Up* is a significant and enduring legacy of this style of film-making, and one that predates the more overtly accepted and desired celebrity that appearances in more recent reality and formatted shows bring.

Between *21 Up* (1977) and *28 Up* (1985) a shift towards a more distinctly observational style is evident, exemplified by Roger Graef's series *Police* (1981) and the BBC2 strand *Forty Minutes*, which ran from 1985–94 under four executive producers: Roger Mills, Edward Mirzoeff, Caroline Pick and Paul Watson. Unlike series such as *Seven Up* or *Man Alive*, *Forty Minutes* was rarely voiceover- and interview-dependent (this is not to say that it did not include interviews, but these were rarely formally framed and shot, as with Molly Dineen's workplace interviews with various people who work at the Angel underground station in *Heart of the Angel* [1989] as they go about their jobs). The *Radio Times* entry for the first *Forty Minutes* ('Rough Justice', produced by Karl Francis) is revealing about the series' intentions:

9.30 *New Series*   31
Forty Minutes
… of documentary. A series of films portraying issues, stories and characters.
Rough Justice. In the Working Man's Institute of Merthyr Tydfil, Dilys Hardacare is up in arms. She's a working woman, but she's still not allowed to join the men at the snooker table. And Howie will soon be in serious trouble. He can't find a job, can't afford to stand his round, and he's beginning to lose his bottle. Around Dilys and Howie, the choir sings. The housewives keep fit and the old men reminisce. Life in the valley isn't what it was. There's no pit in Deri now, and John Jones Treorchy is long since dead. But the humour survives, and it's amazingly peaceful considering …
(On the adjoining page there is a more personal account of the film by its producer.)

This description (more than likely written by the press office, not the programme-makers) emphasises the tendency of *Forty Minutes* to find microcosmic social, personal stories that can be used to represent

Paul Watson's controversial film *The Fishing Party*, broadcast in 1986 as a *Forty Minutes* on BBC2

macrocosmic political structures and arguments. In particular *Forty Minutes* repeatedly demonstrated the potential for wider relevance and signification of the observational form.

Around the time that *28 Up* was broadcast, *Forty Minutes* had entered its heyday with memorable films such as *The Fishing Party* and Molly Dineen's television debut *Home from the Hill* (22 January 1987). Watson's programme, which viewed now seems unbelievably leisurely in its editing and pacing (no music, very little voiceover, languid shots of the Scottish coastline), was a contentious documentary. Filming with four male City friends while on a fishing holiday in Scotland, Watson captured several of the men's unguarded and misguided comments about class, money, race and gender. Those who took part were convinced the film had ruined their lives, and when *The Fishing Party* was re-shown in 2006 as part of BBC4's *40 Minutes On* series, it still had the capacity to shock. As one viewer wrote on the BBC4 'Have Your Say' website:

I must say I was simply shocked at ... the sexist and racist views of the
gentlemen in *The Fishing Party* ... I watched with utter disbelief as their
disdain for human life and utter cluelessness about the human condition
were made clear.

Seven Up offered an alternative though not incompatible way to tackle
comparable problems, often illustrating the human side of a social issue
through its interviews. In *28 Up* the most devastating interview is
probably with Neil, whom we had seen at twenty-one depressed and
living in a squat after dropping out of university, and who at twenty-
eight is drifting around Western Scotland, living off social security. It is
in *28 Up* that Neil is interviewed against the staggering beauty and
ostensible tranquillity of a Scottish lake talking about how he does not
want children as they would be more than likely to inherit some of his
unhappiness and instability. As Moran notes, Neil is inclined in all of his
adult interviews to give his life story a social or philosophical context
(Moran, 2002: 395); he, like Bruce, who repeatedly reminds us of his
privilege relative to the underprivilege of others, draws out naturally the
Forty Minutes tendency to impose general meaning onto the individual's
story. By *28 Up* this has actually become harder to achieve, as it is with
this episode that Apted has started to edit the programmes differently.
With this shift, *Seven Up* – and in this it parallels *Forty Minutes* –
becomes less overtly political and more subject-driven.

    Although the observational mode has rarely been accepted
without criticism in Britain, its overriding interest in ordinary life has
been embraced. Graef's thirteen-part series *Police* was a more authentic
example of observational documentary film-making than *Forty Minutes*,
despite its choices of subject matter, ever was. Graef used film as record,
as with 'A Complaint of Rape', the series' most frequently cited episode in
which the brutal, insensitive questioning of a woman who claimed she
had been raped was filmed over her shoulder to conceal her identity (see
Winston, 1995: 209). But, as Winston stresses 'Graef is in many ways
exceptional' and his practice 'very much at odds with' (ibid.: 210) the
BBC norms of the time, for example, in terms of his high shooting ratios.

33

In the main, the potential inconclusiveness of observational documentary has, on British television, been averted by the imposition of guiding features such as narration, entertainment value or authorial intervention (as in the cases of Dineen or Nick Broomfield). As Winston notes, Graef's work recalls that of Frederick Wiseman; besides Graef, there are many British film-makers (such as Broomfield) who cite Wiseman or the Maysles brothers or Don Pennebaker as inspirations, but relatively few of them who mimic their purer observational style. *The Fishing Party* or *The Leader, His Driver and the Driver's Wife* (1991), Broomfield's portrait of white South African separatist leader Eugene Terreblanche are largely 'observational' in approach but they engineer situations that prompt their subjects to make controversial statements, a significant byproduct of which is their entertainment value, as when Terreblanche gets angry at cameraman Barry Ackroyd and calls him 'a monkey in a bloody tree'.

Despite an enduring preoccupation with ordinary lives, British television documentary has also been equally interested in using or devising ways of telling the ordinary story in an overtly entertaining manner. In some cases the additional factor is humour, in others it is a dramatic voiceover, in some it is undisguised stylisation, which unambiguously signals a film's constructedness. This last approach, for instance, characterised much of the BBC1 series *Inside Story*, whose seasons under Paul Hamann (from 1989) were probably its most memorable. Arguably influenced by Errol Morris's extravagantly cinematic noir-ish style in films such as *The Thin Blue Line* (1988), *Inside Story* became synonymous with the hyper-stylisation of a film-maker such as Chris Olgiati, whose attention to visual style as much as content continued into such series as *Signs of the Times* (1992), Nicholas Barker's groundbreaking dissection of personal taste, and later *Modern Times* (1995–8). Apart from a shared interest in the individual's story with *Forty Minutes*, this is the era when *Seven Up* seems at its most anachronistic as, unlike so many other series (*Inside Story* included), it did not attempt to repackage or reinvent itself.

By the 1990s there were probably more parallels to be drawn between *Seven Up* and other approaches to representing ordinary life. In 1990 *Video Diaries* began in which members of the public with a tale to tell or an opinion to showcase were given a camera and technical assistance with which to put their stories across. It is alongside the innovation of a somewhat 'auto-personal' form of factual broadcasting that the seismic shift that occurred elsewhere in terms of how British television – and the BBC in particular – interpreted the observational, people-based documentary with the interrelated and virtually coincidental demise of *Forty Minutes* and arrival of *Modern Times* in 1995. With hindsight these changes seem significant. *Video Diaries* was self-evidently a diary format and although the series itself has petered out (having been followed for a while by the ninety-second films of *Video Nation*), its popularisation of the ordinary person's video diary has continued into reality television (the '*Big Brother* room') and formatted documentaries (the video links and end-of-the-day video diaries used in *Wife Swap*).

The replacement of *Forty Minutes* with *Modern Times* seems to me to be of comparable significance as it marked the passing of a classically observational strand with one that was always far more preoccupied with style and aesthetics. *Modern Times* was a manifestly 'slavish imitation' (Barker, 1999) of Nicholas Barker's seminal 1992 series for BBC2 about the interior-decorating style and taste of ordinary people. *Modern Times* was launched by Executive Producer Stephen Lambert as a series that considered visual style to be as important as documentary content, an ethos Lambert (who at RDF has been the founding father of formatted documentaries, producing *Wife Swap*, *Faking It et al.*) has continued into later work. It is interesting to what extent *Modern Times* and Lambert's influence more generally have guided what constitutes a documentary strand for 'modern times', as it signalled a move away from primarily content-driven to a far more self-conscious, constructed kind of film-making.[9]

What had altered between *Forty Minutes* and *Modern Times* was not so much subject matter as approach. Barker once mentioned

35

that he envisaged *Signs of the Times* as an extension of the observational tradition established by *Forty Minutes*. What attracted Barker to this mode was its observation of minutiae, the ostensibly insignificant details of the everyday, an obsession that lies at the heart of *Signs of the Times* as well as the portraiture of photographer Martin Parr, to whom the series is explicitly indebted. Instead of reproducing the traditional observational *form*, however, of hand-held camera, minimal director presence and unobtrusive editing, Barker couched his fascination with observing the everyday within a highly self-conscious visual aesthetic, pioneering a reflexive approach to observational film-making that, in a variety of ways, remains omnipresent on British television.[10]

At the heart of the changes that took place in the 1990s in British documentary film-making was a questioning of the traditional relationship between film-makers and subject as a means of understanding documentary's performative base. A more explicit 1990s' example of this is the emergence of the auteur-performer films on television of, among others, Nick Broomfield, who was then mimicked himself by someone such as Louis Theroux. It is not that Broomfield's method was completely innovative (Michael Moore's *Roger and Me* [1989] was contemporaneous with *Driving Me Crazy* [1988], the first film in which Broomfield appears), nor that the film-maker's presence within the reflexive documentary was itself new, as Apted's presence in the *Seven Up* series itself attests. What is significant is that such a reflexive style became so widespread and added to the sense that the documentary genre had in general become crucially aware of its inherent performativity.

In many ways *Seven Up* had always been aware – and had signposted – its own constructedness, for example, through its referencing and re-editing of past programmes, clear indications that 'reality' is a fluid, mutable concept and in perpetuity dependent upon context and contextualisation for signification. There are also the repeated references by many of the interviewees to Michael Apted by name and Apted's personalised voiceover and questioning style ('When we last met …' etc.). The demise of *Forty Minutes* was the result not only of conventional observational programming becoming unfashionable but also due to a fundamental realisation on the part of many broadcasters about the performative nature and potential of documentary: in essence that what is most interesting about documentary is not the idea of a fixed truth being imparted to a largely passive audience but the far more liberating notion of a changeable truth that can be affected by, among other factors, the act of viewing.

The implied presence of the viewing public – whether they are addressed directly in reality shows by being asked to vote contestants on or off programmes or whether their presence is indicated indirectly via an ironic style or voiceover commentary – has continued to be a determining factor for factual programming in Britain. At around the same time as *Modern Times*, docusoaps emerged, with pioneering series such as *Vets' School* (1996). Just as, in terms of strands, *Modern Times* took the place of *Forty Minutes*, so it seemed in the mid-1990s that docusoaps took over more or less directly from traditional observational series such as *HMS Brilliant* (1995) and *Nurse* (1998), both shot on 16mm film over an extended period of time, both made by directors (Christopher Terrill and Jenny Abbott) who 'went native' and lived alongside their respective subjects, and both focused on observing the intricate interpersonal relationships built up within a working environment. There were significant overlaps between such series and docusoaps, as well as equally significant divergences. Docusoaps originated in BBC Bristol under producers such as Nick Shearman – now at RDF Media with Lambert – before spreading to other BBC centres and to ITV (Stephen Lambert, for example, was the BBC's executive producer on *Lakesiders* [1998]). Like earlier observational series, docusoaps focused on working environments and personal interaction (a vets' school, a vets' practice, a driving school, a clampers' office, an airline, a shopping mall, a hotel, a cruise liner), but the balance had shifted. No longer was the emphasis so much on how one learns about the working environment via observation but more on how entertaining people can be when working and/or going about their ordinary business: Maureen in *Driving School* has several near-misses while learning to drive in her Lada; the clampers sing Christmas carols and Jane McDonald sings for the customers on a cruise liner; camp airline stewards act up for the cameras; a hotel manageress and cook have a vocal argument. Complementing this shift, the docusoaps' formal style was similar to that of soap operas, hence the term: they have fast-paced title sequences that introduce the characters in the episode to follow, usually by their first names; the editing style is fast and each episode cuts between two or three individual storylines; the emphasis is on character, emotion and amusement value; all series have a prominent voiceover, often narrated by someone well known and often ironic or patronising in tone.

Ironically, the episode in *Seven Up* that most closely resembles docusoaps in format is 'Seven Up!' itself, which does cut between the children and which does arguably edit their comments and observations (for example Andrew, Charles and John talking through the cons of state-funded education) for heightened entertainment value. Later episodes in the series, however, appear relatively serious and conventional when compared to docusoaps: the editing style from *28 Up* is far less frenetic, as on average each individual story is given around 15–20 minutes; Apted's narration is largely factual (and often remains relatively unchanged from one episode to the next); the primary motive could no longer be construed as trying to squeeze as much instant entertainment value from the interviewees as possible. The principal difference is that docusoaps tend to dwell on people doing things rather than just talking, so they talk as they are performing an action. This is a simple inversion of how later episodes of *Seven Up* handle their subjects, as interviews take priority and sequences of the interviewees doing things (Jackie taking her three sons to the park or John visiting a children's home in Bulgaria in *49 Up*) are largely illustrative. Conversely docusoaps continuously mix action and interview as Jane McDonald in *The Cruise* confides in Chris Terrill's camera while applying her make-up or Maureen Rees in *Driving School* talks about her life as she goes about her cleaning jobs. The docusoap's intermingling of action and interview has the inevitable consequence of diverting viewers from what is being said onto what is being done, a move that has had far-reaching consequences for documentaries since – so much so that in the early 2000s film-makers seem downright wary of using straight interviews, fearful presumably that we would find people talking too dull. Now interviews are too often nervously broken up with reconstruction, music, archive or other diversionary tactics.

Docusoaps, having dominated British television screens for five years, found themselves out of favour almost as abruptly as they had been heralded as the new force in television documentary. The cause of this disappearance is commonly assumed to be the triumphant arrival of *Big Brother* in 2000. The Endemol series was not the only new format around that time, however, for the surprisingly successful *1900 House* was also broadcast (again – in the UK – on Channel 4) in 1999, another key early example of what soon came to be called 'reality television'. What both these series and all the ones that followed clearly exemplify is a triple impulse in contemporary factual programme-making: the need to know where a film or series is going (hence the use of an imposed format or narrative structure, which remains unchanged from week to week); the desire to build into this format a greater level of audience participation; an attraction to documentary subjects not as 'real people being themselves' but as performers who enjoy being on television.

39

The contestants of the first series of *Big Brother* (Channel 4, 2000)

In 2006, the year after *49 Up* was transmitted, *UK Big Brother 7* started; as the contestants on *Big Brother* and *Celebrity Big Brother* get increasingly extreme (soon after the recovering anorexic has been seen crying on *BB7*, two men in a bed with one of the female contestants giggle that they have never groped a pair of false breasts before), so by contrast the interviewees on *Seven Up* start seeming bizarre in their straightness. From having been so intrigued by normality, British documentary has become ever more fixated upon the possibility of playing around with, as opposed to merely observing, ordinariness. This development alters fundamentally our potential relationship with the lives being enacted on screen by making viewers not so much voyeurs sneaking a peek at other people's lives, as if peering through someone's window while walking by, but rather co-creators of performative beings that have only come to life for and as a result of being on television. We are not prying in the same way as we might think we are when listening to the reluctant interviewees of *49 Up* because, as such binaries merge, there is no longer a really concrete sense of the private/public or off-/on-screen divide and private space – what these people might be like when the cameras are not on them – becomes an irrelevance. This process is completed as many of those who have appeared on *Big Brother* and other reality shows rapidly become minor celebrities in their own right, photographed by *Closer* or with their own column in *Heat*.

Although Jackie and others have become more aware of the manipulation (some would say exploitation) involved in *Seven Up* as a result of recent evolutions in television factual programming, their relatively stable presence in the series over more than forty-two years also accentuates some of the differences between Apted's series and reality television. At a recent conference examining the interconnections between art and documentary, Michael Renov observed that the people in documentaries 'do exert a certain kind of pull', a mixture of desire and curiosity which he terms 'epistophilia', concluding that such 'great curiosity' then prompts a series of ethical questions that negotiate and define the viewer's relationship to both that voyeurism and the subjects on the screen:

So then what? What kind of obligations do you have? What kind of responsibility do you bear for that other? I'm interested by the kind of language that artists speak about that level of responsibility, which either you take on or you choose not to take on. (Truth or Dare, 24–5 February 2006, Whitechapel Art Gallery)

I imagine that viewers care in this way for those involved in *Seven Up* much more than they do for the contestants on *Big Brother* or *Wife Swap*, largely because of the impact of being made to realise that these people have lives that, every seven years, are intruded upon. The artificially created environments of reality television serve to repress rather than amplify such an understanding of these individuals' lives.

But to conclude where this discussion began, by making a comparison between *Seven Up* and reality television: one factor that does still link *Seven Up* to *Big Brother* is that they both provide 'water cooler' moments of post-broadcast social interaction. Economist Martin Brookes has remarked upon the positive impact broadcasting can have on '"social capital", the term given to the collection of shared values which shape society and provide the basis for trust between people'. Brookes argues that studies have linked social capital with improved health, reduced crime and better educational attainment and that the growth in the number of television channels and 'the consequent fragmentation of audiences will mean fewer shared experiences, thereby reducing social capital'. [11] The major differences between *Seven Up* and reality shows are on the level of how form and content interact as well as on the level of reception.

In delineating the differences between *Seven Up* and reality television Michael Apted opts to identify the underpinning differences between reality and documentary as a whole:

> In reality people are put into an alien environment and you observe how they react. Documentary attempts to create life as it is, attempts to create life as the film-maker sees it; it doesn't try and contrive it or push it or distort it – it tries to reveal life as it is. That's the idea, anyway. (Apted, 2007)

41

However, these fundamental distinctions notwithstanding, both Apted and Lewis observed during the making of *49 Up* the indirect impact of reality television on how their interviewees responded to being filmed. As Lewis comments:

> When we made *42* there was no *Big Brother*. The landscape has changed for me, between *42* and *49*. In those seven years television internationally had gone 'reality'. I started my research (for *49 Up*) – i.e. chatting to people properly – at the beginning of 2005 and it was absolutely obvious that reality television had made them all extremely wary of doing the film, of saying anything to camera, of being maltreated, or being made fun of. They all said it to me in one way or another. Only one of them would choose to go on a reality programme – Tony, who's an Equity member and would adore to go on *I'm a Celebrity, Get Me out of Here!* ... All the others hate being in the film, they hate the exposure, they hate the invasion of privacy. (Lewis, 2006)

42

How factual television has evolved has impacted directly, therefore, on how those who appear in a series such as *Seven Up* – conceived decades before the arrival of reality television – now define themselves. One potential result of the impact of reality on at least the consciousness of the subjects in *Seven Up* was Jackie's attack on Apted in *49 Up*. This is discussed at greater length in Chapter 3, but the main point of interest for this discussion is that, when Jackie accuses Apted of not having understood her or represented her accurately, certainly Lewis got the sense that the confrontational quality and reflexivity of reality television had influenced Jackie's decision to finally speak out, corroborating Apted's belief that comparisons with reality television were in the minds of his contributors at the time of *49 Up*.

Lewis and Apted have always been sensitive to the accusation of exploitation, in that the children were signed up, in the first instance, by their parents (John maintains that not even his parents but his headmaster gave consent for him to appear [ibid.]) and so did not give their own consent to be filmed until twenty-one. Mindful of this, the series is not, for example, endlessly repeated. *Seven Up* endures in the memory more than it does in transmedia environments and, as a result, several of its contributors refer to the fact that for a few days or weeks after transmission members of the public come up to them or recognise them, but that their notoriety seems relatively short-lived. Herein lies the most significant divergence between *Seven Up* and reality television, namely that while it is generally assumed that the majority of the participants on reality shows get involved because they crave celebrity status, the subjects of *Seven Up* did not. As Nick comments wryly during the montage of interviewees talking about what it is like being involved in the programmes at the end of *42 Up*: 'My ambition as a scientist is to be more famous for doing science than for being in this film. Unfortunately, Michael, it's not going to happen.' It has always been quite a struggle to maintain the interviewees' involvement and the various tensions that characterise *Seven Up*, as well as its familiarity and relative formal stability within a constantly developing genre, are possible reasons for its continuing fascination.

43

3 Textual Analysis

The intention of this chapter is to offer a close textual analysis of the *Seven Up* series with reference, when applicable, to related films and materials. The first section will be about the original 1964 *World in Action* documentary; then I will open this up to include the subsequent series, considering a variety of the issues raised under two overarching subject banners: form and politics.

One peculiarity about researching and writing this book is that, as should be noted at the outset of this chapter, the following analysis stems from having viewed *Seven Up* in a manner that was never intended, namely with recourse to DVDs and/or recordings that can be viewed and re-viewed at will. Any analysis of *Seven Up* based on having watched all the episodes back to back, stopping to take notes and when necessary rewinding, will be fundamentally different from the way in which the majority of viewers will have enjoyed the series, which will have been at seven-yearly intervals. Michael Apted is of the view that the lack of a British DVD of the series is merely the result of 'inefficiency on Granada's part' (Apted, 2007) but, whatever the reason, the series DVD is only available in the US and only the original *World in Action* has to date been aired more than once on British television.[12] The act of watching *Seven Up* for most viewers, therefore, revolves more around remembering than re-viewing.

Of course, people will have recorded the programmes off-air with the intention of re-watching them, but the normal mode of viewing the series has been at seven-year intervals, relying in between on individual and collective memory of what has gone before. Clearly, the series has been edited with this infrequent yet intense viewing pattern in mind and some of the things that might seem repetitious when looking at episodes in tandem, such as the use of the same shots from the earlier films to introduce people (the rather lovely but now very familiar crane shot through a window of an Oxford college to reveal Bruce at a Maths tutorial, for example) or the use of virtually the same bits of voiceover from film to film, need probably to be understood to function as *aides-mémoires* for the rusty viewer.

Because of its iconic status within British television and documentary history, because of its longevity and because it appears regularly but infrequently, *Seven Up* has been of considerable cultural significance and its audiences derive enjoyment from talking about the series as a means of recalling past instalments and committing the most recent episode to memory. I think people also like talking about it out of a nostalgic attachment not only to the proffered image of our own shared historical past but also to its 'children' and the unrivalled personalised social history their interviews have constructed. The randomness of the series – how the children were selected, the individuality of their memories – also in a sense mimics our own experiences of remembering our engagement with a collective past. Only accidentally did our lives coincide with events that might have impacted on the lives of others, and so it is with the *Seven Up* children. It is because the source of many of these memories is the original *World in Action* that I will begin with an analysis of the first programme.

45

'Seven Up!'

As detailed in Chapter 1, the germ of the idea for this *World in Action* Special was the shared fascination with the British class system of Paul Almond (director) and Tim Hewat (at the time of commissioning, series editor). Although the film's UK audience looks at the series from the perspective of being 'insiders' within this system, the *World in Action* film was overtly reflective of the outsider's perspective represented by

Almond, a Canadian, and Hewat, an Australian. This juxtaposition of these divergent perspectives and modes of identification persists to an extent throughout the series, but is most marked in the film of 1964, maybe in part because so much of this first film – the society it portrays, the accents, the images of London's East End, Keay's didactic and gently patronising voiceover, its grainy monochrome image – now seems alien to us. A further consideration is, of course, that 'Seven Up!' was not immediately intended as a series but as a short, polemical stand-alone study of the intersection between two things: the British class structures and the Jesuit maxim 'Give me a child until he is seven, and I will give you the man', the film more or less overtly concluding that an individual's social position is fixed by his or her social origins. As the starting point for the later series, the importance of this first programme cannot be overstated: it remains the moment when the series' view of the children – regardless almost of what these interviewees do in their lives – was fixed.

As the last chapter indicated, the influences upon *Seven Up* and the influence of *Seven Up* are fluid, various and only sometimes predictable. Culturally, texts do not exist either in a vacuum or within neat generic parameters – so *Seven Up* has also evolved independently of both documentary history and of its own impact upon documentary history. As one of *World in Action*'s 'soft' programmes, the original film cannot straightforwardly be assigned to one single documentary or current affairs 'mode': it is not really a current affairs programme in the manner of *World in Action*'s film about the assassination of John Kennedy, broadcast only days after 22 November 1963, neither does it conform to or utilise the tropes of a single dominant documentary style.

A notable feature of the *mise en scène* of 'Seven Up!', for example, is David Samuelson's (and Michael Boultbee's) camerawork, especially for the non-interview sections. Almond recalls coaxing a 'new style of shooting' out of Samuelson, more immediate and responsive than the tripod- or dolly-mounted style of much factual television at the time, for instance, asking him to run after Tony running into school. Almond's memory is that Samuelson considered this to be 'an atrocious

Tony jumping over a fence on his way to school

idea' and thought he would 'get fired as soon as they saw the rushes' (Lewis and Davis, 1991: 7). But the resulting 'fluid camera, following the kids, handheld' (ibid.) worked on various levels, principally as a means of capturing the children's energy by echoing their movements when running, dancing or playing, thereby making their perspective, how they saw the world not just the primary object of interest but the film's subjective core. To return to the example of running after Tony: the film's use of lightweight 16mm cameras for following a documentary subject was one aesthetic feature that made 'Seven Up!' directly compatible with contemporary documentary styles. By 1964, the following the subject hand-held shot (the most oft-cited example being Albert Maysles following John Kennedy in *Primary*)[13] had become shorthand for intimacy – conveying a sense of what it was like to be them. The influence of Robert Drew and Direct Cinema on *World in Action* is also demonstrated by the Maysles having been asked to shoot the American sequences of *Yeah! Yeah! New York Meets the Beatles*, another programme from 1964.

In 'Seven Up!', the pursuit of Tony comes three minutes into the film, part of our introduction to him, an introduction that begins with Keay laughing a little before commenting, 'This is Tony. His girlfriend calls him a monkey.' Keay's tone, the rough camera, the fact that Tony is almost late for school all serve quite economically to typecast Tony as the film's 'cheeky chappy', the favoured role on British television for the East End male. Tony's innate cheekiness is later consolidated by his teacher telling him sternly to turn round and face the front of the class. On several occasions throughout 'Seven Up!', what the camera is striving for is this connection with the children's point of view: sitting at their level, going among them as they dance at their party, filming them up close as they swing round on a rope in the playground, right at the end of the programme.

Lynn at the 'Seven Up!' party

Keay's introduction to Tony is indicative of 'Seven Up!''s style of narration in that it directs the viewers' responses to him, in much the same way as, in the next sequence, the typecasting of John, Andrew and Charles is established in pretty rudimentary fashion via the rendition of 'Waltzing Matilda' in Latin and Keay's voiceover announcing that we have now shifted location to an 'exclusive pre-prep school in Kensington'. The tendency towards stereotyping is most evident in the film's treatment of these three precocious, upper-class boys, wriggling on a sofa, complaining about the Beatles' hairstyles. Again, as with the Tony sequence, the relationship between image and voiceover is fundamental to viewers' perceptions. Perhaps it is the fact that we have already had the sequence at the zoo in which the children were, as Keay states, brought together 'for the very first time' that is conditioning my thinking here, but it seems that John, Andrew and Charles are, in this first film at least, presented to us as freakish animals to be gawped at. Antipathy – or at least resentment – towards the 'posh boys' is insinuated in this opening documentary in various ways. Just after he has declared his loathing of the Beatles' haircuts, Keay confirms 'This is John' adopting a decidedly pointed, irritated tone.

49

Its aesthetic attachment to the new visual style of Direct Cinema notwithstanding, this first film in the *Seven Up* cycle falls most comfortably into what Bill Nichols would term the Expository Mode (see Nichols, 1991). The *sine qua non* of the Expository Mode is the didactic voiceover, as used here.[14] An ironic aspect of the narration in 'Seven Up!' is that, having been written and conceived by outsiders who wanted to make a film about an alien, as they saw it, class system, Keay's voiceover assumes the role of tutor, hectoring and lecturing by implication other 'outsiders' who do not live by or understand the intricacies and inadequacies of such a system. The result is a film that, in critiquing the social delineations that governed Britain in 1964, also reinforces them. There is, for instance, the sequence concerned with the relative merits of freedom and discipline, the starting point for which is a more localised discussion of fighting. After images of two boys boxing in his school playground, Tony at seven affirms the importance of fighting, a prelude to a series of comments from several of the other children culminating in the juxtaposition of two girls – Michelle and Suzy – giving opposing perspectives on the issue, Michelle saying with obvious glee when recounting a tussle with a boy that she 'clumped him one' and Suzy telling a story about a boy who slapped both her and her nanny.[15] This then gives way to the discussion of discipline, starting with Bruce saying 'I think discipline is fair enough' as he is shown being shouted at during cadet training by the prep school 'sergeant', fellow pupil Falmer, who appears to relish his authoritarian role. The implied brutality of cadet training for seven-year-olds is underscored in the subsequent interview with Paul, one of the two boys from a children's home (the ostensible counterbalance to Bruce's boarding school) when he remarks that he does not like 'big boys hitting us', a comment that is then juxtaposed with Andrew's explanation of his school's house captain system.

Bruce during cadet training at his preparatory boarding school

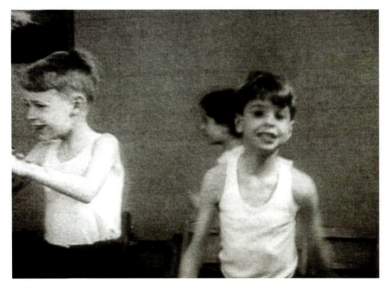

Neil and others participating in a free movement class

51

  Expository documentaries work by having their determinist
viewpoint (frequently explicitly expressed through voiceover)
consolidated at a formal level. Here, the juxtaposition of the fisticuffs in
the East End playground, Bruce and his fellow pupils being drilled and
ordered about by Falmer and Paul's dislike of being hit by big boys
serves to illustrate the implied distaste the film-makers also feel for
fighting. This series of comments and images also, however, moves the
discussion on. After John, Andrew and Charles have argued the pros
and cons of the house-captain system there is a sequence edited around
the general notion of movement and physical play: Neil's free movement
class, Tony in the playground again and Suzy's feminine but regimented
ballet class. This chain of scenes extends the previous focus on fighting
and training but is also used to conclude the film's discussion of
discipline, again through drawing together voiceover and images.
Over the image of Tony in the playground Keay informs us that some
children – that is, unlike the middle-class Neil or upper-class Suzy –

are 'left to amuse themselves', while over that of Suzy practising her ballet positions his narration states: 'This distinction between freedom and discipline is the key to their whole future.'

This is how, classically, an expository documentary operates, by effecting an alignment between formal elements in order to provoke an audience response that concurs with the film's preferred reading of its material. If one views the above sequences in conjunction with the film's overall aim to find among these seven-year-olds the 'managers' and 'shop stewards' of the future, then what is being forcefully implied here is that discipline at an early age is what differentiates those who will assume positions of responsibility from those who will not – and where children fall is entirely dependent upon their class origins.

Linked to this is the later discussion about education in which the children are asked whether or not they aspire to go to university. John, Andrew and Charles map out a clear educational trajectory for themselves (they all envisage going to public school then onto either Oxford or Cambridge, two of them even naming their parents' preferred colleges), while Neil and Peter say they do not think they need to go to university, Neil because he 'doesn't want to be a teacher' and Peter because 'I don't think you need to go to university if you want to become an astronaut.' These relatively informed views on higher education are intercut with three comments from less privileged children: Paul, who asks 'What does university mean?'; Michelle, who says she would like to be like Kathy Kirby; and Tony, who dreams of becoming a jockey.

In 1964 'Seven Up!' notionally set out to construct a critique of the idea 'Give me a child until he is seven, and I will give you the man' but ends up roughly affirming it. The determinist framework of the expository documentary mimics the determinism of this foundational Jesuit belief in an individual's identity; in adopting a didactic documentary structure grounded in the potentially contradictory juxtaposition of an instructive voiceover and contrapuntal editing, 'Seven Up!' ends up reinforcing and fixing the social divisions and problems it putatively sought at the outset to test and challenge.

The trip to the zoo: John tells another boy to stop throwing things at the polar bear

Where Nichols and others are wrong in their negative portrayals of the Expository Mode is in their assumption, however, that such documentaries cannot offer anything other than this rigid, determinist trajectory. Images that mitigate against the fixity implicit in the expository structure ensure that 'Seven Up!' is more than a dated curio: Neil swinging his arms about dressed in his shorts and vest and the close-up of Bruce's troubled expression as he diligently follows Falmer's orders both suggest an individuality that cannot so glibly be made to conform to expectation and type.

There is, if Nichols' theoretical orthodoxy is to be adhered to, a potential discrepancy between the film's attachment to a strong 'voice of god' narration style and its attraction to a messier, more observational type of camerawork or a loosely montage-based editing style. The group outings – to the zoo, the party and the adventure playground – all show that these children 'from startlingly different backgrounds' can both find themselves at odds with each other (John telling the boy in the pork pie hat to stop throwing things at the polar bear 'at once') and able to mix quite happily (Andrew saying, when asked in interview what he thought of the other children at the party: 'I think they were rather nice, really'). The relative freedom of the hand-held camera likewise finds itself somewhat at odds with the more rigid tone of the voiceover, for instance when Keay asks (after Michelle has declared she did not like the posher boys and John has said he found some of the poorer children 'dirty'): 'If some of the children didn't get on with each other, then does it really matter? After all, they're not likely to meet in the same classroom.'

Of Humphrey Jennings's documentaries of the 1940s Andrew Britton argued that Jennings's innate conservatism made him unable to envisage a future that was substantially different to the present (Britton, 1989). In a not entirely dissimilar manner 'Seven Up!' in 1964 framed the future according to the present and ultimately suppressed the more egalitarian potential of some of its own material in favour of boosting its dominant assumption that social divisiveness was here to stay. Although the tone – unlike Jennings's by and large – is critical of the status quo, 'Seven Up!' is far from utopian and like Jennings's films it cannot envisage a future that solves or is free of the endemic social problems it saw. It is impossible now to examine this first film in the series exclusively as an independent, stand-alone programme, although it is most effective perhaps when viewed as such and as a record of Britain in 1964. As Claire Lewis remarks: 'Each film is a time capsule, a place in time which you can't recapture. That's also its value. It's a snapshot of Britain in those seven years' (Lewis, 2006). The 'snapshot' of Britain offered by Almond's film is arguably less rigid in its outlook and interpretation than it might have later appeared.

What has occurred since in the series' treatment and re-editing of the first programme (inevitably, considering the ever-increasing vastness of the project) is that this original stand-alone film has become distilled down to what Apted *et al.* understand to have been its essence.

The cadet-training sequence at Bruce's school, for instance, is never later seen in its entirety, rather it is used as shorthand for the kind of repressive schooling nice, sensitive Bruce had to endure. I am certainly not arguing that, viewed uncut, this sequence constructs an image of Bruce's pre-prep boarding school as fun and libertarian. However, in the boys' inability to march straight or all turn the right way and in their designated sergeant's inability to be convincingly rough with his meandering platoon there does lurk at least the potential for an internal critique of both the school and of the underpinning belief that a child's identity is fixed at an early age. Falmer, after all, is the same boy who, divested of his power, looks rather eager but lost during the Latin class and this cadet training is made to seem more quaint than brutal by virtue of taking place on a rather plush, domestic Hampshire lawn. Of the three gushing letters printed a week after transmission in the *TV Times* of 24–30 May 1964, none of them mentioned the programme's political agenda but all dwelt on the children: 'So wonderfully natural – and the photography of the children so well put over'; 'My heart went out to the two little homeless chaps and the angel-faced one at boarding school whose ambition in life was to see his father'; 'What a refreshing change it was to see those honest, down-to-earth, human beings.' These responses would indicate that, despite Almond and Hewat's best endeavours, 'Seven Up!' could be and was read 'against the grain'. I will now turn to the series as a whole, dividing the discussion into two rough halves: the first examining aspects of the series' form and aesthetics, the second looking at how some of the political issues of this first programme have been pursued and reconfigured in subsequent instalments.

55

Form
Familiarity and repetition

When I asked Apted what for him had been the most memorable bits of *Seven Up* he understandably responded by saying that he could not single anything out, that it was all memorable. He did, though, add that 'The things that appear every time are really the golden bits' (Apted,

2007). I want to start this analysis of the series' form by discussing how these 'golden bits' have been used and repeated and, as a result, have become its defining moments. Both the repetition of the key moments of this first programme – the concluding trip to the playground, for example – and the manner in which its audiences responded to and picked up on its underpinning focus on individuated character signal two key reasons for the series' endurance: the mobilisation of familiarity and nostalgia as mechanisms for accessing and enjoying the series' past and the eventual prioritisation of character and personality over political issues.

The most familiar material from the early episodes is endlessly cited and reiterated: 'Waltzing Matilda'; Nick saying he doesn't answer that sort of question when asked, aged seven, about girlfriends; Bruce saying at seven 'I want to go to Africa to teach people who are not civilised to be more or less good'; Neil saying 'When I grow up I want to be an astronaut. But if I can't be an astronaut I think I'll be a coach driver'; Tony saying ' I want to be a jockey when I grow up'; Lynn saying she wants to 'work in Woolworth's'. The *Seven Up* treasury of such 'golden' moments is plundered endlessly; these sound bites recur so often that they become iconic gestures – not meaningless, but functioning as ciphers or shorthand for the person shown performing them. Such iterations are inherently performative, the signs that summon up the past and render familiar the whole character. This reiteration as opposed to rounded representation of individual histories parallels the act of making *Seven Up* itself, the programmes giving intermittent readings along a continuous curved line. When joined up, these points impart quite a lot of information about each of the 'kids' but they inevitably cannot tell the whole story of the lives in between.

Nick Hitchon, the Yorkshire farmer's son, similarly likened each instalment of *Seven Up*, as Lewis had done, to 'a snapshot'. This comparison with a still, as opposed to a moving, image resonates with the idea that *Seven Up* only offers a limited 'truth': a photo may show a person, details of their lives, perhaps, and how they were feeling at the time the photo was taken – but by its very nature it can never reveal what it might be like to be that person. This conceit of the snapshot as a shorthand rendition of a more expansive life is reminiscent of Judith Butler's notion of gender as instituted in an exterior space through a '*stylised repetition of acts*' (Butler, 1990: 140) and not an internalised 'stable identity or locus of agency from which various acts follow'. Identity in this way becomes a 'social drama', the repetition of gestures performed by and on others. What remains problematic in Butler's writings on identity and performativity is the disavowal of any notion that we as human beings might wish to have and/or retain a sense of our own identity. *Seven Up* is all about the tussle between core identity and the 'stylised repetition of acts': between the children retaining a sense of who they think they are and what, on screen, they have become. Of his own appearances Nick comments: 'It's like DNA: we're all 99 per cent the same. It [*Seven Up*] captures the human condition … It shows what it's like being a human being, not what it's like being me'

57

Nick at Oxford, working in the lab

Nick back on the farm with his two brothers

(Hitchon, 2006) – that is, the 1 per cent that makes each individual different. It is, perhaps, for this reason that several of the *Seven Up* 'children' do not watch their own sections of the programmes as they are transmitted.

Clearly, Nick's acknowledgment of the series' generalised authenticity is entirely compatible with an implicit desire to have chosen a cross-section of society in order to reflect back at society an image of itself. In this sense, the 'snapshot' becomes a reflective image of humankind as represented by a set of individuals. However, *Seven Up* – at least since its structure altered at *28 Up* – has lost or at least suppressed such a political, Lukácsian agenda. Of his practical engagement with the series Nick then says:

> Seven days every seven years, it's very biblical – and weird … You live a completely normal existence for seven years and then they descend on you for seven days. Suddenly you're transported into this alternative universe … a really very special place. (Hitchon, 2006)

To return to the uncomfortable divergence between what appears on the screen and what each of the children would like to see of themselves, Claire Lewis comments:

> People like seeing the film when the image they see on camera is the image they have of themselves. The problem we have is when the camera perceives people maybe accurately, but doesn't match people's perceptions of themselves and that's what happened with Nick and Jackie in *28 Up*. It also happened with Peter and his first wife Rachel. So in terms of portrayal and how people see themselves and talk about themselves, it's all to do with the objective view and the subjective view. We can only ever give them the objective view. (Lewis, 2006)

What ends up on the screen is both – or somewhere in between – the objective and 'a very special place' where who the children are and who they would like to be collide. Nick is a nuclear physicist and he goes on to make a fundamental and enlightening analogy with his own academic field when he says:

59

> There's a rule in physics that you can't measure something without disturbing it, and the same is true with this film. The point is, are we different to how we would have been if they hadn't filmed us? And the answer is a resounding 'yes'. (Hitchon, 2006)

This is a practical as opposed to theoretical definition of the performative documentary act: the performance itself alters everything.

That the 'truth' on screen has a complex, dialectical relationship to the 'truth' that preceded it, that it is not mimicry but performance, is echoed by another of Nick's observations about the types of questions Apted poses and how he answers them. Far from Apted's questions being of the kind that people find themselves being compelled to answer all the time, Nick's contention is that they are totally atypical, the sorts of questions 'nobody I know ever gets asked, certainly not in a public setting'. When I asked him about his experience of being interviewed, Nick responded:

> You get asked a question that you don't normally talk about and then he [Apted] just stares at you, so you just start saying anything. You feel under a lot of pressure to just say something. Stuff flies out of you and the more outrageous it is the more they like it. (Hitchon, 2006)

It is possible that what the *Seven Up* 'children' offer up to the camera, far from being a considered and accurate distillation of who they are and what they are feeling, is a series of occasionally random statements that pop into their heads because of the pressure to say something for the camera.

The process then means that these potentially random iterations establish the basis for the portraits of the children formed by *Seven Up* as well as the foundation for our memory of them. Because *Seven Up* perpetually recalls and recontextualises what has gone before, utterances such as Nick's 'I don't want to answer those sorts of questions', become the statements that, through being serially repeated, are used to sum up each interviewee. This answer of Nick's becomes just such a defining moment, in part because he himself, at fourteen and twenty-one, self-consciously refers back to the way he fielded the girlfriend question aged seven. Part of the pleasure of watching *Seven Up* is discovering what, in the intervening years, has changed, how the interviewees have fared and what they are doing now. However, another huge part of that pleasure is the reiteration of what we already know, the re-use of past moments so familiar that we do not need them to be repeated, really, because we know them by heart. Pleasure, though, is seldom linked to need, as here, when, by *49 Up*, the enjoyment of seeing archive we have seen six times already far exceeds the usefulness of that degree of repetition.

49 Up opens with a montage of the most familiar answers from *Seven Up* including 'I want to work in Woolworth's', 'I want to be an astronaut', 'I don't want to answer those sorts of questions', and at

61

Peter and Neil at seven, smiling at the polar bear

each ad break there is the image of the seven-year-old Neil smiling, looking up at the polar bear in the zoo. How this footage of Neil has been cropped over the years serves as an illustration of how the components that make up *Seven Up* have become streamlined as the series has progressed. Initially, Neil looking up at the polar bear was part of a two-shot, with Peter; however, as Peter has not been interviewed since *28 Up* and as Neil has become the series' mascot – the one who is often given slightly more airtime and who, since *35 Up*, has been put at the end of each episode – so the original image has been modified to reflect this subsequent shift.

Conversely, there are several examples of sequences or pieces of voiceover changing so little that they might as well be lifted straight from the preceding episode. One such instance is Apted's voiceover introducing Tony, running through how he wanted to become a jockey,

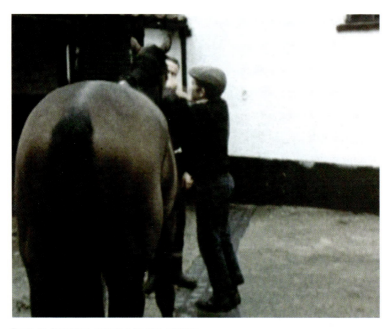

Tony at fourteen working in the stables

at fourteen was already an apprentice at Ronnie Gosling's stables, at fifteen had left school and by twenty-one had not made it as a jockey and was on 'the knowledge', in preparation for becoming a London cabbie. Similarly, the repeated dovetailing of Andrew aged seven mapping out his future educational trajectory ('I'm going to Charterhouse and after that Trinity Hall, Cambridge') and Apted's voiceover reiterating that 'Andrew *went* to Charterhouse, then Trinity College, Cambridge, where he read Law' suppresses the possibility that Andrew might have changed or developed, or done much else with his life except attending Cambridge and become a solicitor. It obviously should not be forgotten that there are seven years between each episode of *Seven Up*, that viewing or recalling the series in its entirety as I am doing here is not only distorting but slightly pathological, but it is nevertheless interesting that the manner in which Tony, Andrew and their fellows are introduced each time is so similar as hardly to merit being re-edited or freshly narrated.

While the series is putatively – yet genuinely – interested in following how its interviewees might have changed with the years, the image sequences of the past that, every seven years, frame each new interview remain largely unaltered. The 'stylised repetition of acts' that make up each individual portrait necessarily limits what we are told or indeed perhaps want to know about each of them so that Andrew *et al.* become defined through and as a series of gestures (possibly arbitrary gestures if others, like Nick, find themselves blurting out what comes into their heads every seven years).

A prominent formal feature of the perpetual negotiation between the established narrative and new material is that the majority of footage used (let alone shot) for each film is only ever seen once. Lewis noted about *49 Up* that very little of *42 Up* was retained, not because it had been a weak episode but because 'of time constraints' (Lewis, 2006). This is undoubtedly true, but it is also the case that the preceding instalment usually features less than the more distant past, and not by any means because what occurs then is more momentous. Each instalment includes a substantial tranche of old material, although the conventional ratio each time is a high proportion of new material to far less old footage, with a bias within the latter towards not only the more distant past but the most familiar images and bits of interview from it. Perhaps because we know the old images so well, the 'past' appears to figure perhaps more prominently than it actually does by virtue of this familiarity. By adopting such consistency *Seven Up!* inevitably finds itself offering a self-reflexive history, with the major source of information every seven years being not the personal histories in their entirety but the potted histories of the previously already edited versions of those wider, messier histories. Apted does, however, have recourse to the outtakes for every film bar the first two because in those cases Granada 'destroyed all material that wasn't in the original films' (Apted, 2007) and so can insert fresh material if it fits.

63

Neil

There are very few cases of previously unseen material being plucked
from the outtakes at a later date and repetition of the familiar is the
series' comfort blanket, the mechanism through which the past (not
heard or seen for seven years) is summoned from the repressed into
consciousness. Some details are not used every time (such as Neil at
fourteen commenting earnestly how hard he's finding it to 'keep up with
the leaders') and one example of something being filmed for one of the
early episodes but not finding its way into the series until a later film
occurs, again in Neil's story, when, at the end of *28 Up*, he is shown at
twenty-one answering Apted's question 'When we come back in seven

Neil playing chess at fourteen, in his East London squat at twenty-one, by
the loch at twenty-eight and being interviewed at thirty-five

years' time, how would you like us to find you?' with: 'In a job, married, probably with children, with a good salary ... and with friends whom I can contact when I wanted to.'

This was not used at twenty-one, but as Neil's situation deteriorates, this fantasy acquires poignancy and resonance. By the time this response is used at the end of *28 Up*, the middle-class ideal that Neil might have been presumed he was working towards is more distant than ever: after searching for him for months, Lewis (then the series researcher) had found him – nomadic, on social security and in North Wales (Lewis, 2006). Neil then moved to the Scottish Highlands, which is where he was filmed at twenty-eight. If any one of *Seven Up*'s individual stories casts doubt on Xavier's determinist certainty it is Neil's. Neil has become, as I have already suggested, *Seven Up*'s talisman – the one who, since *35* has concluded each seven-yearly instalment and the one, therefore, that the rest of the programme is indirectly working towards. After *28 Up*, one impulse for watching the subsequent films was to find out how Neil was, and Apted has frequently played on this, asking in the concluding narration to the first part of *42 Up*: 'And what about all the other children? What's happened to them? Is Neil still homeless? We'll find out tomorrow'. Neil, at twenty-one, dropped out of university and with that turned his back on his apparently steady middle-class upbringing and the expectations that accompanied it. Although it has become the desperate interview at twenty-eight, on the side of the loch, that has become the most familiar, the issues around Neil's mental stability and health first became apparent during his interview for *21 Up*. What I will do here is to use Neil's appearances in *21*, *28*, *35* and *42 Up* as means of analysing the series' narrative structuring of individual stories – the interweaving of past into present and the reassessment that entails, which statements and images are used repeatedly and which dropped, how childhood images are used in conjunction with – or in Neil's case quite often in contrast to – the present.

First, I will examine in some detail Neil at twenty-one, to give an idea of how much new information an individual interview contains, before suggesting how this initial material is edited and re-used subsequently. In *21 Up* Neil comes immediately after Bruce, who has been filmed during his final year at Oxford. The irony of this juxtaposition soon becomes clear, as one of the first things we are told through Apted's introductory voiceover is that Neil dropped out of Aberdeen University after only a term. Apted has found him living in a squat in London doing occasional work as a labourer on a building site and he is interviewed against the window of his room, half obscured by a grimy curtain that has been pinned to its frame upside down. Five minutes into the interview, Apted asks Neil 'What happened?', to which Neil replies, looking defensive and angry as he does through much of this interview, 'Maybe I went to the wrong university, or maybe university life didn't suit me.' The full importance of Oxford specifically is explained a minute later as Neil reveals that he had always harboured a dream of going there:

> It had always been a dream, to get into Oxford. I think people had encouraged me and, because I knew famous people having been to Oxford and I'd read numerous memoirs written by famous people, things such as *Brideshead Revisited*, which was a great favourite. But, these were dreams I had while I was at school. I have to get over the fact that I didn't get into Oxford, probably because I didn't approach the thing in the right way.

The centrality of *Brideshead* to Neil's Oxford fantasy is telling and moving: a novel written from the point of view of a middle-class boy who, upon arriving at Oxford, enters a world of such extreme privilege and brittleness that it consumes and almost destroys him. Neil's tone is always interesting and revealing, frequently oscillating as it does in the *21* interview between detachment (when he talks of his life in more abstract terms) and painful self-awareness and self-deprecation. Here the brighter manner in which he talks of *Brideshead* (that it was 'a great favourite') signals the absurdity of his childish fantasy, before giving way to the morose and introspective way he then ponders the impact of that fantasy as he had not, as a result, approached 'the thing in the right way'.

The poignancy of Neil's situation at twenty-one is further emphasised through being interwoven with the far happier university experience of his school friend Peter, preparing for Finals at London. Peter also functions as the control against which Neil, the other middle-class *Seven Up* child, can be understood and as the one who can go some way towards offering an explanation for why Neil found university so traumatic. Peter has remarked (in response to a fairly loaded question from Apted about whether he was aware of the difference between his background and Neil's and before Neil has started to talk about Oxford) that 'both Neil's parents are teachers ... and that's going to be a hell of a difference ... I think Neil, whether by design or just the situation he was in, was going to be under more pressure'. The contrast between Peter's non-pressurised university

Peter being interviewed at twenty-one in his London digs

experience and Neil's life at twenty-one is emphasised throughout this sequence: Peter preparing supper in his shared student digs in north London, chatting to his flatmates, is juxtaposed with Neil in his east London squat with its dark stairway, cold bathroom and dirty kitchen, which in turn cuts to Peter sitting down to eat his sausages and eggs. This montage concludes with a bit of the boys' 'Seven Up!' interview in which Peter and Neil discuss girls, Neil explaining how the girl Peter's going to marry does not like him. 'Seven Up!' footage of Neil, the luminous, twinkly eyed child of seven, is used repeatedly in *21*, *28* and *35*, when Neil is at his most depressed, unstable and reclusive: visual reminders of what has gone. Later in *21 Up* Neil is prompted explicitly to comment on this change himself, as Apted asks, 'What goes through your mind when you see those films, with you at seven, bright and perky?' He answers:

> I find it hard to believe that I was ever like that, but there's the evidence. I wonder why I was like that? I wonder what it was inside me that made me like that? And I can see that even at fourteen I was beginning to get a lot more subdued, and I was putting a lot more thought into what I was saying, to a ridiculous degree.

Neil here (in *21 Up*) talks about himself over the sepia-tinted image of himself at seven skipping home from school. This is a world apart from where he is in the present and as idealised as *Brideshead*. Neil, at twenty-one, is once more in vision as he concludes

> I didn't have to plan for the future ... because everything was so mapped out for me ... I don't know what sort of stumbling blocks should be put in a child's way to get him used to living in the outside world ... I didn't have enough obstacles to get over.

Asked if he would like to be seven again, Neil replies, with a wry smile, 'No, because I'd know I'd have to be twenty-one again.' It is Neil who

68

draws attention to the fact that he had already changed by fourteen, that the spark had gone from his eyes and that the past, the way he has been brought up, has left a hugely negative imprint. What happens to Neil no doubt compels most *Seven Up* viewers, who might otherwise find themselves nostalgic for the era the sparkly seven-year-old Neil evokes, to realise that the stability of that childhood image in no way guarantees stability in the future. When asked about the 'stability' he has ostensibly 'kicked against', Neil replies:

> I don't think I've ever had any stability, to be quite honest. I can't think of any time in my life when I ever did. I don't think I've been kicking against anything. I think I've been kicking in mid-air all my life.

The image Neil offers of himself kicking in mid-air – reminiscent of Stevie Smith's semi-autobiographical configuration of herself as the swimmer who was 'much too far out all my life/And not waving but drowning' – is repeated in later episodes as a way of recalling his interview for *21*.

69

As a formal demonstration of how *Seven Up* is compiled, the relationship between the ways in which each instalment relates to and reconstitutes the last is revealing about how things are repeated and so why we, the audience, delight in the familiar, in what we have already seen, sometimes several times over (as with Neil saying at seven that he wants to 'become an astronaut'). By *28 Up* Apted has foregone cross-editing, and so Neil's interview stands alone, as it does from this point on. What I want to do now, having talked about the traumatic moment of transition in terms of Neil's life trajectory, is to offer a diagrammatic interpretation of how the interviews for each *Seven Up* film relate to and incorporate each other, up to *42*. For the purposes of clarity, I have only mapped out in detail the use made later of material from Neil's interviews for *21* and *28*:

28 Up	35 Up	42 Up
From *21 Up*: 'I've been kicking in mid-air all my life'	→ used again	→ used again
'I didn't have enough obstacles to get over'		
Oxford dream (shortened)		
'Maybe university life didn't suit me'		
'I don't think I was really taught any policy of living at all by my parents'	→ used again	→ used again
'I'd like to be someone in a position of importance … I always thought, well, I'd love to be in politics …'		→ used again
Looking back at himself at seven with disbelief		
Does not know if he believes in God		
	From *21 Up* interview, but not previously used:	→ used again
	Qu: 'When we come back in seven years' time how would you like us to find you?'	
	Neil: 'In a job, married, probably with children, with a good salary … and with friends whom I can contact when I wanted to.'	

From 'Seven Up!' and 7 Plus Seven:		
'I want to be an astronaut'	→ used again	→ used again
'We pretend we've got swords'	→ used again	→ used again
'We play international wrestling'		
Comparing city living to country living	→ used again	→ used again
'I want to travel'		
'I don't want to have children'	→ used again	
'Coloured people'		
'I believe in God'	→ used again	
'It's hard to keep up with the leaders'	→ used again	→ used again
	From 28 Up	From 28 Up:
	Asked if he worries about his sanity	→ used again
	Talking about being on the dole	→ used again
	'The days seem long'	
	'You finish the week, you come home, you plug into the TV set for the weekend and then you manage to get back to work on Monday. It seems to me this is a slow path to total brainwashing'	→ used again
		'I'm not claiming that I feel I'm in some sort of nirvana. I'm just claiming that if I was living in suburbia I'd be so miserable I'd feel like cutting my throat'
	'I always told myself I would never have children ... because children inherit something from their	

71

| | parents and even if my wife were the most high-spirited and ordinary and normal of people, the child would still stand a fair chance of being not totally full of happiness because of what he or she would have inherited from me' | |
| | 'How's God been treating you?' | |

In two significant ways Neil, despite his story being atypical, exemplifies the formal conventions of *Seven Up!*. The first of these is that the childhood images used for each interview remain largely the same, no doubt in part due to Granada having destroyed the outtakes of both 'Seven Up!' and *7 Plus Seven*. In Neil's case the juxtaposition of childhood and adulthood, as discussed in relation to *21 Up*, is particularly emotive, because of his nervous disintegration by twenty-one,[16] and it is certain key images of him – especially aged seven – that recur every or almost every time, that are used to emphasise this. Over the years these have become increasingly detached from their original context, transformed instead into instantly readable signifiers for a contented childhood, hence the regular, but not especially informative, repetition of the story of Neil and Peter playing with swords. The significance of Neil wanting to become an astronaut or of recounting his bouts of international wrestling are not in themselves nearly as significant as the manner in which they are told and what they convey about Neil: his smiling eyes, his delight in talking or in embellishing a story.

Of more significance in terms of content specifically are the selections made from Neil's contribution to *7 Plus Seven*. Because at fourteen he had started, in hindsight, to display some of the neuroses that emerge later (and Michael Apted has remarked that it is only when he interviews Neil for *49 Up* that his eyes have started to twinkle again

[Apted, 2006]), *7 Plus Seven* is more directly relevant to Neil in adulthood. At twenty-eight, having admitted that he still occasionally thinks about having failed to get into Oxford, a sequence of an earnest Neil playing chess at fourteen (not used in *21*) is placed in the middle of a portion of interview that continues:

> I don't think I was half as clever as I thought I was. Unfortunately, I grew up against a background of people of pretty average intelligence. I don't think I went to a school full of bright people. If that had been the case, I don't think I'd have been so big-headed. I know I went to university expecting to be something of a genius, and found that wasn't the case at all. Which is a good thing for me.

Chess in this context becomes Neil wanting to appear clever. He is also modest, so when Apted tries to get Neil to confirm his intelligence by revealing his A-Level results he refuses, saying simply 'Yes, the grades were quite satisfactory').

The second way in which Neil is revealed, in the above diagram, to be a representative *Seven Up* contributor is in how, in each instalment, the present takes precedence over the past, especially the immediately preceding episode, which is, in the main, edited back to its bare essentials. Although the interview for *21* is, in Neil's case, mined relatively extensively, the motivation for this is clear: Neil's life had, seven years earlier, taken an entirely unexpected and negative turn, and repeating a higher proportion of *21* is suggestive of the continuity between that and *28*. What occurs later – and this is more arbitrary and instinctive than logical – is that *28 Up* becomes for Neil the defining film, particularly the most powerful moments, such as not wanting children because of what they would inherit from him and others worrying about his sanity. Maybe the centrality of *28 Up* in later episodes was because it proved that *21* was not a blip (as it turned out to be with the equally unhappy Suzy), or maybe it was because it had been at *28* that the *Seven Up* production 'family', as it is now constituted, came together or maybe it was because the interview with Neil for *35*

73

Up proved so 'unwatchable', as Lewis terms it, in a way that the one for *28* – against the water on a crisp, bright day – for all its tragedy, was not. Of the interview at twenty-eight Lewis says:

> He was so ill we could only interview him in short bursts because he couldn't really talk for very long ... and we stood there, Michael and I, in tears. We said 'Oh my God, it's every parent's nightmare. What happened, what went wrong? How do you take a child who is like that at seven and is hardly functioning at all (by twenty-eight)?' (Lewis, 2006)

Neil is ostensibly even less well at thirty-five, although he is, as Lewis observes, able at least to live in a community (in the Shetlands). Whereas he rocked back and forth at twenty-eight, at thirty-five his face is covered in sores and he is suppressing tears throughout, as if the interview is not just emotionally but physically painful. More so than in *28 Up*, he also distances himself from his own words and from what Apted is asking of him. When, for instance, Apted asks the inevitable question 'Do you ever think you're going mad?' and Neil's reply is, 'Oh, I don't think it, I know it. We're not allowed to use the word "mad" but I think most people are mad here really, but then I think it's a mad world.' Neil moves swiftly here from seeming as if he is about to treat this interview as therapy to detaching himself from his personal predicament, even treating it with a certain irony as he talks of 'a mad world'. This distancing occurs repeatedly in Neil's interviews throughout the series and when this detachment is not there 35, as Lewis intimates, does become virtually unwatchable. Its concluding sequence is Neil in an island pantomime, barely able to hold himself together, having answered Apted's standard question, 'What are you likely to be doing [in seven years' time]?' by admitting, 'That's a horrible question. I tend to think the most likely answer is I'll be wandering homeless around the streets of London. With a bit of luck that won't happen.' Then intercut with the panto, he continues: 'I know how tempting it is to escape into fantasy ... but the most difficult thing is to accept the reality, to be what we are in a situation we're in, that's terribly difficult.' The theatre curtain comes down on this, with only the ubiquitous playground sequence to detract from the pain of watching Neil's tortured performances.

The nuances and layers of such a sequence can never be repeated in subsequent films; each instalment of *Seven Up* is thus totally unique. Just as most of each film subsequently ends up on the proverbial cutting-room floor, so only what might be deemed to sum up one episode, to capture its essence, is preserved for later; and what remains of *35 Up* – and indeed *28 Up* – by the time *42* comes around is very little, bar the obligatory sequences from each in which Apted asks Neil about his sanity. The viewer's understanding of Neil at forty-two, however, is not simply based on the repeated sound bites, but on at least some sort of residual memory of the detailed sequences now omitted or pared down.

The unexpected

Out of this discussion of how certain of Neil's contributions interrelate and interweave, I want now to move on to examine how *Seven Up* more generally negotiates the unexpected, as ostensibly the unpredictable or unplanned event does not fit its Jesuit schema wholly unproblematically. Any documentary film or series that follows a predetermined structure becomes especially interesting at points of surprise, shock, disruption, when the format is challenged. Obvious major disruptions are the decisions by some of the 'children' to cease taking part in *Seven Up* and how the series integrates these in each case. Just as Apted's narrated introductions to each of the remaining people have become standardised, as the series' interview style has with time become equally conventionalised. As Lewis remarks, she and Apted, in advance of filming, 'draw up a long list of questions' many of which cover the same area each time (marriage and partners, children and family, work, health, spirituality recur frequently): 'We call it money in the bank, because you never know when you're going to need those answers' (ibid.). However, for most of the time the 'children' change remarkably little from film to film; as Bruce comments, 'it seems odd how the characters are quite set from early on', although he also doubts Xavier's maxim and wonders if 'people can be that manipulated' (Balden, 2006). Reflecting this, the filming procedure also remains generally consistent, with Lewis having spent time with each contributor and having gained a sense of what has been going on in their lives prior to filming. As Bruce attests, the crew then spends two days with him filming 'a variety of activities – lessons, games at work, then with the kids at home' including a Saturday 'if Penny wants to be involved' (ibid.).

Occasionally, something comes up during those filming days that neither Apted nor Lewis were expecting. One such incident is Tony's confession of adultery at the start of *42 Up*, which Lewis describes thus:

> The interview at forty-two was terrifying. I was sitting under the table at the time. I knew they weren't getting on. Debbie is feisty and smart. It was almost as if Tony had to confess to the world what he'd done to try and make amends. But we didn't know that was coming and our mouths were open. I was sitting under the table thinking 'Oh my God' and we carried on filming as it got more and more awkward … Tony's always said to Michael and me 'You can ask me what you want, I trust you.' (Lewis, 2006)

Tony at forty-two confessing his adultery, with Debbie beside him

The resulting spontaneity of the exchange with Tony – with Debbie interjecting 'You got caught, and that was that', Apted asking her why she chose to forgive him and Debbie then remonstrating 'I've never been unfaithful ... I feel I'm a good wife and didn't deserve it' – contrasts significantly with (and as a result sheds doubt upon) the excessively familiar introduction with which Tony's section opens.

Another incident – this time that Lewis knew about in advance but Apted did not – was Jackie's attack on Apted during her interview for *49 Up*, prompted by Jackie remarking that her son Lee's temper is a trait he has picked up from her and Apted, seemingly innocuously, responding by asking her if her temper has ever got her into trouble. Jackie fires Apted a look and retorts 'You're probably the best person to answer that', prompting a cut to an argument they had during *21 Up*, in which Jackie objects to Apted's suggestion that she has 'settled down' too young. The sound fades out and Apted, at the time of *49 Up*, can be heard to say 'I like it when you shout at me', to which Jackie's annoyed response is 'I'm not sure you do really.' Jackie, at forty-nine, then refers to the moment, at twenty-one, when Apted had asked her if she had had enough experience with men before getting married: 'I thought that was an insulting question and I got very angry, and we actually stopped filming because of it.' She then goes on, referring to the filmed material of her at twenty-one: 'To all intents and purposes, I might as well not have been there. I was really angry ... You wouldn't have asked some of the other people in this programme that question.' In the midst of this is a brief shot from *21 Up* of Jackie with her head bowed, not looking at Apted or towards the camera, archive that, in the light of her later tirade, a viewer sees as pointedly significant. The forty-nine-year-old Jackie looks towards Apted, angry and defiant. This is an engrossing moment of self-reflexivity. What is interesting is seeing on camera the unrehearsed renegotiation of Jackie and Apted's relationship. Beforehand Lewis had reasoned with Jackie that 'it's really no good you telling me these things, you've got to say them to Michael on camera' (Lewis, 2006). Although, as Apted has said, 'Looking back, it was probably on the cards' it still came as a

77

'shock – not just to me but to the crew, the way she went for me' (Apted, 2007). Apted concludes that 'Of course she has a point', because what Jackie questions ultimately is the act of documentary film-making:

> Anyone who thinks there's anything pure about making a documentary film is delusional. Every edit is someone's judgment. Someone has to make that judgment – in this instance me – so that becomes my view of the world. She's right about that. (Apted, 2007)

Now, in the era of reality television and formatted documentaries, such performative moments have become commonplace, but in referring outwards to the filming experience of *21 Up* as well as to her relationship with Apted, Jackie is also critiquing the cosy familiarity that, by *49 Up*, had built up. Jackie continues:

Jackie at twenty-one following her argument with Apted

You definitely come across as this is what you want to do, how you see us – and that's how you portray us. This one may be, *may be*, the first one that's about us rather than your perceptions of us.

This extension of her argument prompts Apted to ask in reply, 'So how up 'till now have I got you wrong? … What would you like to talk about?'

Jackie's section culminates with her replying, 'I think I'm more intelligent than you thought I would be … I enjoy being *me*, but I don't think you ever really expected me to turn out the way I have.' To an extent in 49 the unexpected and potentially disruptive element becomes assimilated; reflecting on what it has been like being part of *Seven Up* informs more than Jackie's interview, but it also comes to influence Apted's interviewing style, as he starts to ask other contributors to talk about their participation. For Apted, however, there still remains a fundamental difference between reality television and *Seven Up:* 'the whole essence of reality television is to contrive a situation … I choose not to contrive; I take a chance' (Apted, 2006).

The peculiar conjunction of contrivance and chance has led to various surprises in *Seven Up*. Jackie now has three sons, for example, two of whom (James and Lee) were born between 35 and 42, which has balanced out rather neatly the oft-repeated tale she recounted at seven that her mother had seven years' bad luck so she had five girls. At 42, after an introductory montage comprising the seven years' bad luck story, Jackie as an adult saying repeatedly that she did not want children, the revelation in 35 that she had had Charlie but does not 'want Charlie to be an only', we see Jackie preparing breakfast. The framing is sufficiently tight that it does not to give away who is sitting round the table, so at the beginning of the sequence it is not known how many children Jackie now has. She brings over one bowl of cereal, which we discover is for Charlie, then another for James and finally a last for Lee. After this gradual revelation – a repeated trope of Apted's and one that here he manifestly relishes – Apted asks 'What's the most fun?', to which Jackie responds 'The sheer unexpected pleasure of them.' This is not merely an illustration of the bringing together of contrivance and chance, but of content and form, as Jackie's expression of the unexpected joy of motherhood echoes the pleasure derived from holding back on revealing the unexpected to the *Seven Up* viewers.

Also in *42 Up* is the defining unexpected moment of the series to date: the revelation not only that Neil is not homeless on the streets of London as he had predicted at the end of *35* he would be, but that he had become a Liberal Democrat councillor for Hackney and, after *35 Up*, had been befriended and given a place to stay by Bruce. Although Michael Apted does not presume to think that the series has fundamentally changed who these people are (Apted, 2007), there are instances – such as the friendship between Neil and Bruce – that would not have come about if not for the series. Those involved in *Seven Up* have an existence related to and to some extent dependent on the series and are occasionally brought together outside the context of filming, for example, as a group at theatrical screenings of each instalment or for the premiere of one of Apted's other movies (such as the UK premiere of *Amazing Grace* in 2007 [ibid.]). Bruce describes the atmosphere of *Seven Up* screenings as immensely supportive:

> When we meet up we tend to be pleased to see each other and tend to support each other as each person's bit is shown … Then we tend to go for a meal or a drink as a group. (Balden, 2006)

The only person he has got to know personally, however, is Neil, who is godfather to his eldest son Henry. For the viewer who has made an emotional investment in *Seven Up*, the friendship between Bruce and Neil is probably especially poignant: Bruce the upper-middle-class boarding-school boy who talked frequently of wanting to help others and become a missionary and Neil, who tangibly needed help. *42 Up* shows many of the interviewees to be particularly content. At thirty-five, Apted had asked Bruce (*apropos* of being single), 'You're getting on a bit, are you worried?', to which Bruce had replied, 'Not particularly,

Bruce's wedding to Penny in *42 Up*

I mean who knows what might happen tomorrow?'. In *42*, the next
image is of Bruce getting dressed for his wedding to Penny, as Bruce's
voice from *35* continues 'That's the trouble with reserve. You never
know what might have been.'[17] Apted comments how well these
moments 'play' when one of the 'children' do something they have
previously sworn they would never do or looked extremely unlikely to
do – Suzy, at twenty-one adamant she does not want children and
happily married with two sons at twenty-eight, for example (Apted,
2007).

During Bruce's segment for *42 Up* there is no reference made
to Neil, and the section on Neil opens with another ironic juxtaposition
of past and present, after the familiar montage and a long recap of *35
Up*, which culminates in Neil predicting that, in seven years' time, he
will be homeless on the streets of London, 'but with a bit of luck that
won't happen'. The next image is of Neil, in coat and trilby, walking
towards Hackney Town Hall, the sequence then cutting to inside the
council chamber where Neil is making a speech. Not only has Neil

81

manifestly defied his own depressing predictions, but he has also fulfilled his ambition of becoming a politician – an ambition he had espoused in his squat at twenty-one (this clip is shown again here), but that then seemed a distant fantasy. Then, a minute or so later, the other big revelation – Neil's friendship with Bruce – comes, again built up not through pre-emptive voiceover but through images: of Bruce and Penny's wedding, at which Neil is speaking. Bruce then explains, over images of the wedding guests, walking along the street back to his house for the reception, that after the dinner for *28 Up* he had said to Neil that he could kip with him; Neil then subsequently stayed with Bruce for two months after coming down to London from the Shetlands.

Steve Neale, in his discussion of melodrama, uses Franco Moretti's argument that audiences are moved to tears in certain narratives at the moment when one character is brought from a position of ignorance to one of knowledge, but only when this revelation has come too late and the tragic or melodramatic situation is irreversible, tears thus being the product of the audience's powerlessness (Neale, 1986: 8). A specifically documentary-based conjunction of elements moves us to tears in *42 Up*, centring on the melodramatic coincidence of what really happens to Neil and Bruce on several levels (that Neil is not homeless and has entered politics, that he and Bruce are friends and that Bruce is now married) coinciding with our imaginative fantasies of what we might have wanted to have happened to them, a level of personal engagement with the series amply demonstrated by the number of people who wrote to Apted after *28 Up* offering Neil work and help. The unexpectedness of the Bruce and Neil story in *42 Up* stems not merely from the classic reversal of fortunes both experience but from this rare conjunction of factual (and thereby unpredictable) event and (more predictable) audience fantasy. *49 Up* in this sense disappointing, for although both men are still happy, they have lost touch since Neil moved to Cumbria, sometimes exchanging cards at Christmas, but little else.

Journeys

That Bruce and Neil have not kept in touch is one indication of the unpredictable nature of the journey that *Seven Up* has undertaken: several documentaries are 'journeys', some more overtly so than others. *Seven Up* is an example of a documentary made over a long period and has been an exceptionally long-term undertaking.[18] It is also an open as opposed to a closed journey in that, despite its definite sociological beginning, it no longer possesses a complementary endpoint in terms of what the factors will be to draw the series to a close. The interplay between this narrative openness and the series' more familiar elements is important, as each film pursues and observes action rather than dictates it. The journey *Seven Up* undertakes can be broken down into various smaller journeys: the interviewees' life cycles, the viewers' accumulated knowledge of them, the growing familiarity between the interviewees and Apted, the reassessment every time of the past through knowledge of the present. The impulse to construct fixed narratives is, according to Hayden White, an impulse 'so natural ... that narrativity could appear problematical only in a culture in which it was absent' (White, 1987: 1). To White, the impulse to defy the omnipresence of narration is perverse and illogical, but it remains what, to an extent, drives and liberates a longitudinal documentary such as *Seven Up*. Formally, it is built upon a paradox in that the form it takes is predictable, but its content innately haphazard (as Apted has remarked, he 'takes a chance'). Bill Nichols, in the mid-1990s, argued that while traditionally 'documentary' as a term,

> suggested fullness and completion, knowledge and fact ... more recently
> ... documentary has come to suggest incompleteness and uncertainty,
> recollection and impression, images of personal worlds and their subjective
> construction ... What counts as knowledge is not what it used to be.
> (Nichols, 1994: 1)

Within the *Seven Up* series a similar shift occurs in terms of 'knowledge' and how it is imparted; as the longest-running documentary series, it has clearly undertaken a significant historical journey, but it has undertaken an aesthetic journey as well. Apted has argued that the series 'has stopped being a political document and has become more of a humanist document ... The series doesn't disown politics, but deals with politics via character' (Apted, 2006). This shift is in part a formal one, as itemised in Chapter 1: *World in Action* set out to make a film with a specific and didactic socio-political agenda (Keay's voiceover in particular attests to this) and is structurally confrontational in that the children were deliberately chosen to represent the polarisation as Almond and Hewat saw it of British society at the time. The political agenda and social juxtaposition were at this point underscored by the use of contrapuntal editing, as it continued to be until *21 Up*. *28 Up*, as I have already mentioned, established a different editing style as each individual story was separated out and shown sequentially. With this move, the supremacy of the interviews over all other material became overtly stated, and the journeys through these people's lives became almost exclusively articulated through what they have said about themselves.

84

The interviews are shot simply. As Apted elaborates:

> I had a feeling early on that it would be best to do these films very simply. The biggest card I'd have to play would be those faces changing over the decades ... I always concentrated on a static interview, and although I did a certain amount of 'B' roll, I didn't let it dominate, because I felt if this went on ... the clarity of the thing was important ... I have to think of the next episode every time. (Apted, 2007)

The most evocative *Seven Up* 'journey' is the one we can see in the faces of the interviewees; not merely the ageing process and the natural transition from childhood to adulthood, but also how expressions, feelings and responses change. The issue of knowing, before filming begins, that, all being well, the film-makers will want to return again for another interview in seven years' time is a crucial burden that 'most documentary film-makers don't face' (Lewis, 2006). Apted corroborates this when he comments that, 'It's very different being in this longitudinal game, because you have to behave yourself'; the relationship with his contributors is always delicate because they have 'much greater power over the film-maker' than most documentary subjects and,

> If I put things in they don't want, or I do things they've asked me not to do, then they're likely to say to me that they're not going to do this again … there has to be much more give and take between the subjects and the film-maker on longitudinal work. (Apted, 2007)

That the future perpetually informs how the film-makers are working in the present is a peculiar and no doubt stressful imperative to work alongside.

The manner in which Apted poses interview questions is crucial in this respect. Although Nick Hichton (cf. above) has characterised the questions as difficult and quite unlike the sorts of questions one would normally be asked, others talk of Apted's interviewing style differently. Lewis, for example, remarks that 'Michael's interview technique is superb; there's no side to him. There is no catching out involved'; the ethos behind the technique is equally simple:

> All we want to do is find out how people are at that particular point in their lives and what they think about things. That's it really. They choose or not to tell us. Whether they tell us the truth or not we don't know. (Lewis, 2006)

The aesthetics of the interviews reflect this straightforward intention, as Apted suggests when he remarks that his 'biggest card' is these faces that change over time. Very little interferes with our engagement with the interviews in *Seven Up*. They are framed simply and shot on a tripod-mounted camera that occasionally and unobtrusively zooms in or out; neither the editing nor the lighting is ever ostentatious or self-consciously drawing attention to itself; each interview is shot by and large in an unremarkable location; and (rare for contemporary documentaries) there is no extra-diegetic music.

Complementary to this is Apted's relative unobtrusiveness. Although these interviews are essentially conversations and his questions remain audible, he is more a facilitator than an interrogator. As Bruce comments:

> I don't think he likes the sound of his own voice, in both senses: like the rest of us he's probably a little embarrassed about how he sounds and also he doesn't want to be too intrusive. He wants the other person to tell their story and he'll prompt. There's not much of a sense of dialogue between him and me or whoever else it is. It's more reflective. You don't have a vivid impression of hearing him a lot. (Balden, 2006)

The minimalism of this style draws attention to the rapport between Apted and his interviewees, which in turn raises issues about the documentary journey and the perpetual tension between past and present that each interview or each programme enacts. The major element of this relationship (which Lewis and others have commented on) is the trust the contributors to *Seven Up* place in both Apted and Lewis, hence the latter's likening of the filming process to a family reunion. Apted configured this trust in an interesting if slightly tangential way when he raised the question of age difference. Apted is roughly fifteen years older than the *Seven Up* 'kids', but as this has, with time, 'diminished' in significance, so 'the whole way they regard me has changed, and the whole way I regard them' (Apted, 2007). He has gone from being the 'big brother' or 'parent/teacher' to being their 'colleague' and as a result, 'the more we do them (the programmes) the closer the relationship is, which makes for a more intimate and frank exchange' (ibid.). Although Apted does not consider his interviewing style has changed much, the content has because 'we are much closer to each other than we were when they were fourteen and I was twenty-nine – that's a big, big age difference, a whole cultural divide' (ibid.).

Politics

Over the course of its long history – and particularly after the switch
from a dialectical to a linear structure from *28 Up* on – *Seven Up* has
become less intrinsically political and, in this respect, to recall Bill
Nichols (quoted above), what counts as its knowledge 'is not what it
used to be'. Not altogether as a result of this shift in editing styles, the
political agenda that drove the original *World in Action* film has been if
not obscured then dissipated. Whereas Almond's initial film overtly
pursued a political agenda, Apted's subsequent instalments have become
less self-consciously reflective of British social politics. A certain amount
of political discussion still takes place – Neil getting elected as a Liberal
Democrat councillor, John still hoping, at forty-nine, to enter politics,
Bruce's consistently socialist affiliations – but it is not foregrounded to
the same degree. Although there have been instances when the political
emphasis of the first programme has been reintroduced, such as the
epilogue to *42 Up*, when the interviewees are all asked in turn whether
or not they think Britain is still a class-ridden society, the series has
become, as intimated by Apted, more interested in the politics of the
individual.

    In many ways the life trajectories of the 'children' continue to
tell us quite a lot about the politics of the time. Through Neil's
biography, for example, we could chart a particular middle-class story:
the aspirations towards educational success, the inability to handle
disappointment resulting from these aspirations not being fulfilled, the
workings of the social benefits system, the shifts in party politics since
the 1990s. Likewise, Nick's story is somewhat the reverse: the boy from
the Yorkshire Dales who goes to Oxford and is now a tenured professor
in a top American university. Apted acknowledges that some have
criticised the series' lack of topical, political references, but argues: 'I do
know that when I've tried to be contemporary or have tried to make the
film political, it has never worked. It's never made it even into the film
I did it in, let alone into times future' (ibid.). When shooting *42 Up*, for
example, he asked the contributors about the then recent death of

Diana, Princess of Wales, but in the end did not use any of the material. Politics in *Seven Up* are conventionally more generalised. The following analysis of the relationship between politics and *Seven Up* is subdivided into three categories: class, humanism and gender.

Class

Talking about how the children were selected for the original *World in Action*, Michael Apted has remarked that he only realised 'much later' that,

> maybe the original choice had been politically self-serving. But Granada had wanted to make a political point about the British class system, which I was happy to go along with. We chose the kids from the two extremes of society, which rather proved and argued our point. (Ibid.)

This, twinned with the desire to test Xavier's maxim, put issues of class and upbringing at the forefront and set the agenda for *Seven Up*. As Joe Moran identifies, 'The principal aim of bringing together children from "startlingly different backgrounds" ... was to show the impact of class distinctions on life chances' (Moran, 2002: 388–9). Lewis adds about this first film: 'the middle-class as we know it was completely not there, partly because it wasn't there in 1964 ... The only middle-class representatives were the two Liverpool boys, Peter and Neil' (Lewis, 2006). Compounding issues for the series' analysis of class have become Peter's absence since *28 Up* and the fact that Neil is so atypical.

There are various things – not just the middle class – that 'aren't there' in the *World in Action* film, such as most of Britain. At several points Douglas Keay's voiceover draws attention to the programme as a portrait of contemporary Britain and as offering 'a glimpse of Britain's future' and yet there is one boy from Yorkshire, two from Liverpool and one girl whose father owns a large swathe of Scotland and apart from that the children selected are from the South of England. There is also only one non-white child (Simon) and just four girls. Unlike some subsequent series that have mimicked *Seven Up*'s format, *Seven Up* itself is not centred upon a cross-section of British society, but as Apted acknowledges an agenda-led selection that could be accused of being 'self-serving'.

The working-class children come, on the whole, from a well-defined and familiar social group centred on London's East End. Half a century on from when the series began, this 'East End' is rarely talked about regularly or adhered to as a valid social configuration, except perhaps in *EastEnders*. At the outset of *The Uses of Literacy* Richard Hoggart argued that one of the issues, when attempting to define what was meant (at the end of the 1950s) by 'the working classes', was trying to avoid 'the romanticisms which tempt anyone who discusses "the workers" or "the common people" ' (Hoggart, 1957: 13). Romanticism colours how the Londoners are portrayed in the first *Seven Up*, and the nostalgic image of the 'East End' as a predominantly white working-class

89

The old East End from 'Seven Up!'

cockney-speaking ghetto was, even in 1964, blinkered. In "*Fires Were Started –*" (1943), for instance, made about twenty years earlier, the new middle-class fire-service recruit asks directions to his City posting from a Chinese gentleman. The transition from white to multiracial East End is emphatically signalled in *49 Up* at the end of Tony's story, when images of the vibrantly coloured market stalls and curry houses of Bangladeshi Brick Lane are juxtaposed with Tony, a self-defined 'traditionalist', bemoaning the fact that the East End has changed, that the pubs are closing and everyone 'wants their own culture'. Less than ten minutes later, Jackie evokes the same old East End when, talking about the Scottish housing estate on which she lives, she mentions that she likes it because, in its neighbourliness, it is 'like the East End used to be thirty years ago'. The view of London's East End constructed in the earlier episodes was commensurate with what Jackie is nostalgic for here: Tony's Saturday mornings at the pictures, the washing hanging on the line, Lynn declaring she wants to work in Woolworth's and Jackie herself saying, without hesitation, that if she had lots of money – 'say £2' as Sue formulates it – she would give it to the poor and hand out food at the harvest festival. It was also commensurate with crime and Apted's conviction, early in the series, that Tony would turn to crime and follow in the footsteps of the Krays (that in *21 Up* he is asking Tony if many villains live in the East End as Tony is driving him down Vallance Road, where the Krays lived, makes this very obvious). As early as twenty-one, though, Tony is asking Apted to revise his narrow view of the people of the East End. Having been asked if he regrets not having had a good education, Tony gets increasingly tetchy and counters:

> I'm as good if not better than most of them people – especially in this programme. I mean, I'm one of the tailenders. You'll think 'East End boy, he ain't got no good education', but he's got a car, a motorbike and goes to Spain every year. I've worked for it.

Tony's strong attachment to the East End (and to a clichéd East End at that – immediately after saying the above he is shown dog racing in

Hackney) has also, over the course of the series, compelled Apted to reconsider the stereotypes associated with it. That the East End has become less white and less working class is demonstrated by Neil and Bruce living for several years in Hackney – and the images of nearby Brick Lane look like they have been extrapolated from Bruce's sequence in 42.

The first film idealised the East End of Tony, Jackie, Sue and Lynn over and at the expense of its social opposite, represented by Suzy, Bruce, John, Andrew and Charles interviewed on their comfortable sofas and chintzy chairs. This is the series' underpinning binary. Aged seven, and immediately after Jackie has declared that she would give her £2 to the poor (thereby not bracketing herself as poor), Simon is asked what he thinks of rich people to which he replies 'not much … Well they think they can do everything without you doing it as well.' This, in turn, is immediately juxtaposed with John saying about the poor: 'I don't think much of the accents', before both Charles and Andrew criticise their own class for boasting and teasing poorer children. The class distinctions between these children at seven seem sharply defined and the children acutely aware of them, although this is also the result of how questions have been put to them to draw out this social thesis.

A fundamental issue with the series is that the working-class contributors in particular refuse to unproblematically and explicitly define themselves in class terms. Jackie, for example, from the age of seven has offered a nuanced and complex image of the English working class. In 42 Up, in between pieces of interview in which she talks about being a single parent who would find it hard to cope financially without the assistance of her mother-in-law, Apted has inserted Jackie at seven saying 'If you didn't look after the poor they'd die soon', the inference presumably being that the same could be said of her. To the end of this interview – which only latterly reveals that she has had to give up work due to rheumatoid arthritis – Jackie refuses to seek our sympathy, closing with: 'I am down and I'm depressed about my illness but I'm certainly not down and depressed about my life. I'm lucky. There's a lot of people a damn sight worse off than I am, a lot worse.' Just as Jackie

91

does not necessarily stick to the series' 'social script', as Joe Moran refers to *Seven Up*'s reinforcement of certain fixed class-related expectations, so Simon, like Jackie, deviates from his 'script', arguing in *42 Up* that he 'stopped thinking about colour a long time ago'. Just because Jackie is 'working class' and Simon 'black' does not mean that it is through this that they define themselves. The premise of the original programme might have been prescriptive in this way, but the subsequent films allow for the problematisation of such imposed and narrow definitions. As Moran argues: 'It is not that class becomes irrelevant in the later programmes of the series, however, but that it is seen as working itself out in complex ways' (Moran, 2002: 391).

Tony opened the montage at the end of *42 Up* with the idea that class still could make a substantial difference – that someone might get a job because 'daddy goes to the right club', but his view is countered by most of the others: Andrew, directly after, comments that, when recruiting for jobs in the city, 'social distinctions have become less important'; Jackie argues that it is money and not class that gives you an advantage (an issue that came up during the film as she in passing compared her life with Suzy's) and Neil concludes that 'the only excuse for class is ignorance'. *Seven Up* as a series has offered a long, though fragmented and erratic portrait of Britain over the past fifty years and one of the social changes it has witnessed is, if not the dismantling of the class system, then the blurring of class differences, and in particular the redrawing of the original conceptualisation of the British 'working class' as an amorphous group. Over the course of the series, though issues of social background still feature heavily among Apted's questions, the working class comes to be seen more as comprising a group of individuals. In part, this is the result of the younger generation going against the stereotypes and being released from the disadvantages that dictated to an extent the lives of their parents. Although Sue says at twenty-eight (under a barrage of questioning from Apted about the impact on the three East End women of class differences), 'I think we all could have gone in any way we wanted to at the time, within our capabilities', and although Lynn is entirely supportive of her daughters' decisions not to go to university, *Seven Up* increasingly signals the relaxation, the erosion of class stereotypes. The shift is signalled in, for example, Paul in *49 Up* talking about his daughter being the first member of his family to go to university, a proud revelation that Apted pointedly juxtaposes with Paul, aged seven, asking 'What does university mean?'. Likewise *49 Up* is the first film in which the three East End girls are not bunched together, finally released from a falsifying sense of homogeneity.

The extent to which the 'children' appear stereotyped, even into adulthood, is in substantial part the result of the initial methods of and reasons for selection. Inevitably the children in the original *Seven Up*, through being repeatedly juxtaposed, were seen and judged against each other, meaning that any information gleaned is the result of the dialectical opposition of individuals representing what the original programme-makers understood to be the social extremes of society in 1960s Britain. However, despite the dissipation of this inherently political structure as, at *28 Up*, the films' structure changes, not many of the ways in which, in the *World in Action*, social differences were delineated are subverted or altered. None of the straightforwardly working-class children selected went on to university, for instance. This valorisation of 'going to university' as a barometer of class, though not arbitrary, is a fixation of the film-makers and seems to be particularly important to Michael Apted. That Suzy did not go to university appears to be less of an issue for Apted than it does when he questions Lynn about her daughters, as Suzy is not perceived as needing to 'escape' her class. If other determinants of social standing are adopted, then the differences evident in the original programme are no longer so clear-cut: that the working-class kids did not go to university does not automatically mean that they are financially disadvantaged. Tony, for example, has two houses by the time *49 Up* comes around and Apted asks Sue, 'So, have you moved up a class now?' as he surveys the home she has bought with her new husband, to which Sue replies 'It feels like that to me.'

Nick never conformed easily to the series' early stereotypical conception of the working class. Although selected, as Nick himself puts it, as 'the one from the lower-class rural family' who would contrast neatly with Suzy, 'the upper-class rural' whose father owns 'tens of thousands of acres of Scotland, apparently' (Hitchon, 2006), Nick's 'success' is that he went from a one-room primary school to the 'local grammar school', then on to Oxford to read Physics, ending up Professor at the University of Wisconsin, Madison.[19] Conversely, the other grammar-school child in *Seven Up* is Lynn, who in the end chose not to continue into higher education.

Nick still feels (despite Apted's frequent assertion that he is the series' 'success story')[20] that *Seven Up* pigeonholes him and finds it impossible to deviate from the motive for selecting him in the first place, and that 'anything that doesn't quite fit what he (Apted) wants to portray of me doesn't play' (ibid.). Nick, though, articulates the tensions and ambivalences in having left his 'lower-class rural' background. On the one hand, going to university was tantamount to 'class disloyalty' and being bracketed alongside *Seven Up*'s upper-class kids – whom the series portrays 'so negatively' – made him uneasy; on the other, Nick is proud not to have been limited by his background. This equivocation recalls Hoggart's description of 'the scholarship boy' in *The Uses of Literacy*, who has 'a sense of no longer really belonging to any group' and who is 'declassed' and 'at the friction-point of two cultures' (Hoggart, 1957: 292). Nick remembered being told about a lecturer at teacher training college who concluded, after watching *7 Plus Seven*, that 'it was clear that this fellow (that is Nick) ... will never get anywhere educationally', then surmising that what the programme was saying was that 'if you're a kid going to a rural school it's either that you're uneducable or that you're not going to be given a fair chance by the system' (Hitchon, 2006). Ultimately, due to time restrictions perhaps, *Seven Up* has tended to emphasise certainty and suppress ambiguities and contradictions. One irony that does not come out, for example, is that Nick's father had gone to university, so for his son to do the same 'wasn't such a huge leap' (ibid.).

Of the fourteen children, the ones from affluent backgrounds are Bruce, Suzy, John, Andrew and Charles. Various other factors link these children besides wealth, exclusive education and social expectations, such as the fact that the majority of them lived through their parents' divorces in their childhood or teens. But these, within the series' political schema, become tangential. It is when editing and talking about the more privileged children that Apted seems especially attached to the notion of a 'social script'. He does not assume they should live that script, as becomes clear in *21*, as he introduces Suzy with the words 'This is Suzy – the product of a private education and wealthy parents', before revealing her, having left school at sixteen and gone to secretarial college, to be deeply unhappy, chain-smoking and extremely reluctant to answer Apted's questions. With the boys, the script – coupled with their ability to follow it – is at its strongest. That the three boys continue to be bunched together in the films further strengthens this view of them as conforming to class expectations.[21] The series has been harsh on these three and, as Lewis remarks, 'I'm constantly surprised that more of them haven't said no' (Lewis, 2006). To date, Andrew and John still agree to be interviewed, although John refused to do *28 Up* because of how he was portrayed in *21*: 'which was hunting and shooting and fishing in a derogatory sense' (ibid.).

95

Apted's criticism of the three posh boys is, though, only implicit; there is a certain distance between him and them, a coolness of tone, a sense that he does not know them in the way he knows Jackie or Bruce or Neil. In John's case, the lack of intimacy and understanding is undoubtedly also due to it having been Lewis and not Apted who has conducted the interviews with him for *35* and *49 Up*, (he did not appear in *42*). Any detachment from the three boys, however, does not automatically translate into explicit criticism on Apted's part, which is reserved almost exclusively for those with whom he seems more generally sympathetic and emerges at those moments when he feels people have failed themselves and, above all, their natural intelligence.[22] For instance, in *21 Up* asking Simon, after a sequence in which he is shown working in a meat factory, 'Don't you ever feel you should be doing better than this? Aren't you worth more than this?'. Neither Simon nor Neil, when asked a similar question, agree with Apted's assumption that they could do 'better' or that they are 'better' than others. Apted is also intermittently critical of Bruce, asking him if he lacks ambition, and of Tony, who again is asked at twenty-one if he feels he has failed in life because he failed to become a professional jockey. This is a particularly critical interview, and Apted turns to Tony at one point and remarks, 'You're very short', an observation – coming from Apted who is not short – that momentarily deflates even Tony.

As John took particular exception to his portrayal in *21 Up*, I will now look briefly at the three boys' contribution to that film, also because it was the last time Charles agreed to take part. The boys are interviewed both as a threesome and separately. The sequence opens with the iconic discussion between the three seven-year-olds regarding which newspapers they read. This, like the rest of the old footage in *21*, is sepia-tinted and is juxtaposed with the three of them at twenty-one sitting on another sofa reflecting on the series' value. John argues that at seven they did not know very much, to which Andrew adds, 'We didn't know very much when we were seven, but we were still quite funny.' Charles rather more lumpenly interjects, 'All we can do is say what we think and if they're [the viewers] interested in it then good luck to them.' In setting out to use the three posh boys reflexively, Apted is, as a matter of course, distancing them, using them to carry on a meta-discourse on the value of *Seven Up* as opposed to getting them straightforwardly to divulge details of their current lives. From this point on it becomes increasingly clear that Apted is directing them to talk about specific issues, most importantly education, what they want to do and tradition. John remarks (now being interviewed in his student rooms at Christchurch, Oxford) that 'parents have the right to spend their money as they see fit', that car-factory workers 'earning huge wages' could equally well afford to send their sons to public school, they just have different 'priorities' and choose to buy 'a smart car' instead.

After having him at seven predicting he would go to Trinity Hall, Cambridge, the voiceover starts off the section on Andrew's education with 'Andrew is in his last year at Trinity College, Cambridge, reading Law'. Andrew continues John's discussion about the value of

John interviewed at twenty-one

John hare hunting at twenty-one

of this sequence, John is being set up not merely as the upper-class boy who, having been put on the 'conveyor belt' Charles describes, ends up at Oxbridge with all his cronies, but more broadly as the traditionalist who stands for a whole set of anachronistic and elitist attitudes.

The targeting of John is achieved via editing and contextualisation. The sequence, though not overtly distorted, is biased, for although John says all the things he does about fathers who work in car factories being able to afford public-school fees, that here he is positioned so effectively as the embodiment of Charles's production line is a narrative construction made doubly significant by the fact that the simile echoes John's allusion to the well-off car-factory worker on *his* production line, shoving out cars at the end, soon to be emphasised again by the interview with Simon, who works in a meat factory. The hare-hunting sequence continues, as does John's individual interview, in which he declares himself to be 'reasonably old-fashioned'. He goes on to voice

John, Andrew and Charles interviewed together for *21 Up*

his dislike of the 'permissive society', 'decreasing respect for the family unit', 'dishonesty' and the diminution of 'personal integrity', all the result, as he sees it, of the encroachment of the 'American way of life'. Apted posits that John could find himself 'isolated' because of his views, to which John's response is that he does not mind, that what is important is that he does 'what's right'. Just as it was the interweaving of image, interview and voiceover in Paul Watson's *The Fishing Party*, which led to such a negative portrayal of those four wealthy men on their Scottish fishing holiday, so here it is the juxtaposition between images, John's interview, Charles's words and ultimately the transition to the sequence centring on Simon and Paul, the two boys from the children's home in Middlesex, that creates such a critical portrait of John. His positioning at the extreme end of the upper-class spectrum is sealed with each three-shot of all of them on the sofa: Charles in his worn sweatshirt, turned up jeans, lank hair and high-lipped tan-coloured leather shoes; Andrew in his anonymous dark two-piece suit and tie; John in his more flamboyant three-piece Prince of Wales check tweed suit and brogues, proclaiming his old-fogeyness. John is the traditionalist who considers it to be his patriotic 'duty' to stay in England and give something back to the country that has privileged him to such a degree. He, at twenty-one, is being set up; a couple of furtive looks directly to camera, especially at the end of a zoom into a close-up of his face, suggest a certain wariness on his part and a belated sense that he knows this to be so.

    The framing, camera movement and lighting during this sequence complement the ideological tendencies of the editing – that the camera just as frequently moves *out* from a close-up as vice versa, thereby distancing us from the subject; that John perceives the interview to be antagonistic and not friendly; that the three of them (perhaps with the exception of Charles for his individual interview) are placed against functional and cold backdrops (literally in Andrew's case, who is interviewed on the piste). Conversely, the interview with Neil at *28 Up* is not memorable just for its content but also for the tender golden light, the beautiful setting and the contrast between shadow and light that bring us closer to Neil, make us more receptive to him.

Although no one would contest that John, at twenty-one, said what he is shown to say on camera, his anger at how he is represented in *21 Up* is legitimate in that he is more or less explicitly set up as representative of a particularly privileged, traditionalist stratum of the upper classes. It is all too easy to keep watching *Seven Up* over the years and to think that John never changes substantially, that his identity was solidifying at seven and fourteen and fixed by the age of twenty-one. That the 'posh boys' are being utilised in *21* as proof of the rigidity of the English class system becomes clear as they are prompted to discuss reflexively the point of the series and how they are represented in it. It is the case that, even aged fourteen, the trio takes on the role of those who most overtly question the programme's agenda. John asks, 'Is the point of the programme to reach a comparison? I don't think it is ... We're not necessarily typical examples ... there's an attempt to typecast us', before Andrew concludes, 'so everything we say they'll think "Oh, that's a typical result of the public school system" '. The continuation of this meta-discourse consistently distances us from John, Andrew and Charles and constructs them as particularly stereotypical representatives of their class. Our perspective is thus linked to Apted's slightly cold and critical view of their conformity and class solidity.

Bruce and humanism

Later in *21 Up* comes the bulk of the interview with Bruce, in his final year at Oxford reading Mathematics. Bruce has always stood apart from the other three privileged boys and, in tandem with this, has always been treated differently. As a seven-year-old interviewed on his own, Bruce seemed more vulnerable than John, Andrew and Charles; at fourteen, as he talked about the lack of snobbery at his new school St Paul's and his Labour leanings (that he would have voted Labour at the last election if he had been eligible and that he 'didn't agree with the Conservatives over what they were doing with the black people'), he was maturing into a humanitarian socialist. By the time *21 Up* comes around, it is evident that, as an indirect response to this innate sensitivity, Apted's attitude is to let Bruce talk more about himself and less about how he fits into the class system. This is a significant shift as, unlike the 'three posh boys', he is no longer being forced to conform to an imposed archetype. Given more time within the programme than many of the children, Bruce, at twenty-one, divulges that in his gap year he taught at a school for the 'handicapped' (although he is reticent to talk about this and is only nudged into doing so by Apted), saying he enjoyed it but not necessarily because of the 'slightly charitable nature of the work'. To this, Apted responds by asking: 'Why are you frightened of presenting this image of yourself?', leading Bruce to say, 'Possibly because I never want to feel too proud ... I can pretend to be humble, but that's being proud in a different sort of way. I find it difficult to avoid pride.' If Neil is the most emotionally and psychologically complex of the *Seven Up* 'children', then Bruce is the saintly one and in terms of the series' dissection of the class system functions rather neatly as the control figure with whom it becomes increasingly evident Apted himself identifies and with whom the audience is invited to identify as well.

This identificatory pattern is confirmed a little later in *21 Up* as Bruce explains his interest in politics, joking that he is the only socialist in his village and duly expected to defend everything socialist in the pub, saying he is 'still a socialist, but not as energetically as I was' before going on to talk eloquently, before Margaret Thatcher came to power in 1979 (*21 Up* was transmitted May 1977), about the problem of the Conservatives wanting to bring back the notion of freedom:

> I'm glad the socialists are in power because this elusive thing called 'freedom' is sort of rearing its head and the Conservatives are pushing it forward and I thought this argument was smashed in the early years of this century but it seems to be coming back and it really is exceptionally dangerous because the more you try and defend freedom the more you allow everybody to do exactly what they like ... there's no freedom in living in a slum. It's all right, you can say, the chap can do whatever he wants, he can get a proper job ... but that's just not the case. The more you defend freedom the less you have it.

101

Bruce here is, in certain respects, answering John speaking some twenty minutes earlier, saying that the car-factory worker could afford to educate his son privately, but chooses not to. Although the order in which the pivotal statements about class, work and education appear in *21 Up* (John followed by Simon and Paul, then Tony and finally Bruce) already conveys to an extent Apted's perspective, his identification with Bruce is confirmed midway through this section with Bruce as he can be heard emitting a kind, understanding laugh as Bruce describes the tenor of his socialism.

Bruce himself is interesting on Apted, talking about how he has softened over the course of the series, in the process revealing quite a lot about how *Seven Up*'s discussion of class and politics has likewise mellowed. Despite the similarities between Apted and Bruce (that 'in terms of our outlooks we're similar' [Balden, 2006]), Bruce also notes that Apted is

Bruce at twenty-eight teaching in an East End comprehensive

> a very driven man ... very ambitious, and I think to begin with he was
> always looking to see where people had got to and said things like 'You're
> just teaching in a school again?' and that kind of thing. He's mellowed a lot
> and that's made the programmes more reflective and less of a polemic.
> (Ibid.)

Bruce is appreciative of the fact that *Seven Up* represents him positively,
that 'they're always pleasant to me, and the things I've regretted saying
they haven't shown', citing as evidence that it would be just as easy to
do the opposite and follow Richelieu's maxim, 'give me six lines by the
most honest man and I'll find something therein to hang him' (ibid.).
To a significant extent the personalisation of Bruce, the humanist
response to him, allows this otherwise classic representative of the
privileged classes to transcend and not be confined by the series' self-
imposed socio-political schema. Apted is occasionally hard on Bruce (but

Bruce learning Bengali in Bangladesh

as I have suggested, his harshness is often reserved for the contributors with whom he feels more comfortable), as when, at twenty-eight, he asks Bruce if he has 'any sense of disappointment' about ending up teaching in Tony's old school in the East End, having been to 'a major public school' and Oxford, or at thirty-five, when he enquires 'You're getting on a bit, are you worried?' after Bruce has referred to the fact that he is not yet married. Most of the time, however, Bruce is handled generously.

Such generosity is mimicked at a formal level when, at *42 Up*, there is the fairytale conclusion to Bruce's romantic solitariness (he had joked at thirty-five that he did not 'want this to turn into a dating-agency video'), as he is shown marrying Penny. *42 Up* is the logical conclusion to Bruce's portrayal to this point as liberal, saintly and not necessarily conforming to class expectations. Bruce had also paved the way – augmenting the formal change at *28 Up* towards editing the stories individually – for a shift in emphasis from ideological intent to humanist interest. Apted had not anticipated *Seven Up* would be the success it has been in the US. As Lewis comments:

> Michael used to always think it was parochial and always resisted the film being theatrically released because he thought American audiences wouldn't understand it. He was absolutely wrong about that. It has found common ground wherever it plays because it's essentially about people and everyday things. (Lewis, 2006)

Apted's initial concern was that audiences from outside the UK would see it merely as a film about the intricacies of the English class system (Nahra, 1999: 22); after *Seven Up*'s success in the US and elsewhere, he revised his opinion and consistently began to attach the term 'humanist' to it, commenting to me, for example, that,

> It's stopped being a political document and has become more of a humanist document. The series honours the ordinary life; it deals with things we all deal with ... The series doesn't disown politics, but deals with politics via character. (Apted, 2006)

The construction of a social portrait of Britain via this relationship between politics and character is arguably *Seven Up*'s most significant political as opposed to aesthetic intervention, although it is extremely important also to remember that, as a social portrait, the series could have been as effective if made using an entirely different selection of children. As Apted suggests:

> I'm thrilled how this lot turned out, but what I have to believe the film does in a sense is honour the ordinary life – that people who have ordinary lives as opposed to celebrity lives can be very articulate and their lives can be full of changes about which they'd have a lot to say. And I think that would have been true whoever I'd chosen. (Apted, 2007)

The series' depiction of Bruce makes the idea Apted raises in the first of the above quotations of dealing with politics via character particularly pertinent, as Bruce's life trajectory and interviews at seven-yearly intervals comment indirectly and directly upon the changing British political landscape: what socialism has stood for in this country, its and its replacement with a brand of Conservatism based on the valorisation of the individual over society, the changing face of London's East End, the divisiveness of our education system etc. It is obviously not only Bruce who works in this representative way, as it is through all the individual stories working themselves out over years and decades that the series' social history of Britain emerges. It is, though, through Bruce's life in particular that an audience is likely to get nostalgic for 'true' socialism, for the breaking down of the rigid class distinctions that were shown in the original *World in Action*. Although documentary film-maker Adam Curtis has argued in 2007 that in Britain the divide between rich and poor is greater than ever and that social mobility is now far harder than at any point since World War II,[23] Bruce's story is one of the individual narratives that conversely puts across the notion that the impact of class on the individual has, over the years, lessened. Bruce's life and his articulation of his political views combined offer a positive rendition of liberal humanism, the preferred ideological tendency of the latter part of

105

the series and so his emergence as *Seven Up*'s 'control' figure – the one against whom the others are measured, the one who offers the most universal point of shared identification – is concretised.

That is until *49 Up*, perhaps, when Bruce has left his job at an inner-city comprehensive to take up a post at St Alban's School, an exclusive public school in Hertfordshire. At this juncture Bruce stops being a representative figure who embodies social and political struggles and reverts to being the interesting individual. It is at forty-nine that Bruce arguably and finally proves Xavier's maxim. Apted opens the section on Bruce in *49 Up* with the now familiar montage of his past life: declining a verb in Latin, talking, at fourteen, about the relative lack of snobbery at St Paul's, solving a Maths problem during an Oxford tutorial, teaching in London at twenty-eight, in Bangladesh at thirty-five, back in the East End at forty-two, running the Maths department at a girls' school. Then, the image cuts to Bruce singing in the school choir at St Alban's Abbey, the voiceover furnishing details about the school (that it was founded in 948, for example) and that it is a boys' independent school that takes girls into the sixth form. The inherent beauty of the sequence in the Abbey is significant here as it helps to convey why Bruce might have made the decision to opt out of state education, a move that prompts Apted to ask if he is compromising his political principles. Although one has to read between the lines a bit, it is clear from Bruce's reply to this that he no longer felt comfortable putting these 'principles' before contentment, that those who could dedicate their lives to teaching in inner-city comprehensives were saintly. Apted here inserts a resonant image of the East End school's waterlogged flat roof, which in turn feeds neatly into Bruce's next comment, his recitation of the motto 'Water weareth away a stone by dripping on it.' Bruce interprets this as first a metaphor for teaching and then as a metaphor for himself. His first thought was 'you'd keeping teaching, eventually it would get through', subsequently realising it was he whom the water was wearing away. Bruce says frankly now that he had come to the conclusion: 'I don't think I can do this until I'm sixty.'

This sequence concludes with an edit that affirms the transition Bruce has made, as Apted cuts from an image of Bruce in the East End with one of him walking towards the Abbey in his gown. Although he jokes that friends give him a hard time, accusing him of having 'joined the Tory party, the golf club, the Masons', Bruce also appears extremely happy, remarking that at seven he looked 'lost and a little sad' and that, at forty-nine, 'I'm quite surprised to be contented and reasonably happy', a realisation rounded off by another shot of the idyllic village cricket match in the glowing summer sun. There is a significant fusion here between tone, content and visual style, as Bruce himself suggests when commenting:

> The other thing he's (Apted) doing, which probably has a lot to do with George (Jesse Turner) the cameraman, is that the films look pretty good. There are some lovely images just of me playing cricket. The way they filmed it made it look idyllic. I had no idea we were in such an idyllic setting ... I also noticed how beautiful Bangladesh looked (in *35 Up*) and other bits where Neil was in the Highlands or Cumbria last time, how nice everything looked. (Balden, 2006)

107

Bruce's section in *49 Up* concludes with Apted asking him what his dreams have been, to which he replies that he would have liked to have been an international cricketer, then adding: 'I think we just live without our dreams.' On the surface, Bruce's comment is about his childhood fantasy of sporting success, but as a comment that could have an interpretative role beyond the immediate context, his abandonment of his 'dreams' refers perhaps to his decision to stop living his socialist ideals. Bruce's reversion to type seems in some measure to be a desertion. Lewis talks eloquently about the conflict when it comes to Bruce between our fantasies of what we, the audience, might want him to represent and what he actually as an individual person is and does: that through our impulse to identify with the children in *Seven Up* and with Bruce in particular we fantasise about him becoming the 'flag-carrier' for all social idealists. Bruce said, through becoming a teacher at an inner-city comprehensive,

'I've thrown away my background, I was privileged, I went to public school and Oxford, I had all this and I stayed here.' But actually it's all real. We have no control over these people's lives and they do what they're going to do. And it's that touch of reality – for me it was Bruce saying he'd learnt to live without his dreams – that made it (*49 Up*) absolutely real ... it's that disappointment, it's that moment of pathos. (Lewis, 2006)

In terms of the series' examination of the class system, as Lewis concedes 'people have turned out more or less as you thought they would have done, given their backgrounds', that although,

the working-class kids have all done very well individually ... the upper-class kids are still the opinion formers. They're the lawyers, the solicitors, they're the ones on the side of the people running the country and if John decides to run for parliament before *56 Up* he *will* be running the country.

Lewis concludes that 'the class issues' are now significantly 'blurred, and the films are now about individuals. But if you look at the bigger picture, I don't think anyone has moved outside the area where you'd have expected them to be' (ibid.).

Women

Where we would expect the *Seven Up* children to have ended up is most manifestly an issue with the girls – Jackie, Lynn and Sue from the East End and Suzy, their upper-class counterpart, who, in *49 Up* signed off and will probably not be interviewed again. The issue around expectation and gender is acutely felt among the production team because there have been so many significant problems caused by the inclusion of so few girls back in 1964.[24] Lewis noted, upon being given the researcher's job on *28 Up*, that, although the series to date displayed an acute awareness of class issues, 'we were desperately short of women and, to be perfectly honest, up until *21*, there wasn't really any great awareness among the production team of "Oh my God, we've only got

Lynn stamping
children's books in the
mobile library

Sue and her children

109

Jackie and her eldest
son Charlie

four women in this" ' (ibid.). Lewis then goes on to recount an early exchange with Apted on the subject, remembering how she asked him where the women were, to which Apted responded honestly along the lines of 'In 1964 that was never an issue'; so, as Lewis surmises, the original *Seven Up* 'is as much a reflection of the time when that film was made as of the individuals within it' and Apted, by *28*, realised the situation was 'dreadful' (ibid.). The way Apted and Lewis chose to redress the gender imbalance as much as they could was by interviewing the spouses and partners of the men 'particularly Australian Sue and Tony's Debbie became relatively major players in the piece' (Apted, 2007). The inclusion of these women, however, runs counter to Apted's aspiration to 'keep the film very focused' on the individuals and their stories and not to tamper with the series' established format. As he continues: 'I've avoided on the whole using children ... and I've tended to avoid husbands because I don't need more men' (ibid.). Despite this increased awareness of the series' gender imbalances, it was only with *49 Up* that Jackie and her friends ceased being grouped together for interviews.

110

Tonally, the successive interviews with the three East End women are compelling. First, there are – perhaps because both groups are threesomes – similarities between how the 'girls' respond to Apted and how the three 'posh boys' do. Underpinning (or undermining) the interviews with the two threesomes is a latent sense that these people have lost some of the individuality attributed to the others; they are asked questions collectively quite often and are, reciprocally, presumed to hold similar views. In part because Andrew has, on occasion, been the only 'posh boy' who would consent to being interviewed, this is less of an issue for the boys than it has been for the three women. It is also that the lives of the three women have followed similar trajectories in that they all married young, two had children relatively young and all have children now, that their home/work balance has been such that individual careers have not dictated what they have done with their lives. There is an oft-repeated line uttered by Lynn at twenty-one, when she recalls a headmaster telling her at school that she and her friends would not amount to much, that their only aspirations were to get married, have kids and push a pram along the street 'with a fag hanging outside your mouth'. As much as the three upper-class boys, the three working-class girls are sensitive to issues of pigeonholing and of what is expected of them, both from Apted and from society. It is not so much that the three girls do not fit the series' ideological schema, which in some respects they do, but that they consistently demonstrate an awareness of what is expected of them and why they are being asked certain questions.

I have already discussed Jackie's argument with Apted at *49 Up*, in which she takes issue – after years of silent resentment – with the manner in which the series has hitherto represented her. The argument to which she refers took place when she was twenty-one. Elsewhere in this same interview one can see Apted again stereotyping the girls as he asks them (having intercut Suzy's interview with theirs) whether or not they resent the disparity between their lives and Suzy's. Jackie again reacts strongly to the suggestion that she should want what Suzy has and Lynn argues that she has more than Suzy because 'she's been so conditioned into what she should do and what she shouldn't do'. Apted invites these sorts of reflexive responses from one interviewee about another infrequently, but in *21 Up* the question about Suzy forms part of a wider discourse on what privilege can and cannot offer, as Suzy – miserable, cynical and chain-smoking – is the very obvious product of her parents' unhappy marriage and subsequent divorce. The three East End girls come from more stable, contented homes, so they did have something Suzy lacked.

The same question, however, is asked of Jackie, Lynn and Sue at twenty-eight, when Suzy – as viewers already know – is far happier: married, with two small sons. Lynn again becomes the spokesperson as she comments: 'In some respects I think the boys and Suzy didn't have such an open choice as we had. It was mapped out from such an early age as to where they were going … it's a hard thing living up to parental expectations.' Here, the argument becomes more nuanced as Jackie, for example, concedes that a 'comfy background' can make life easier;

111

however, what is significant is that the trio of women again seems to be the ones (rather like John had done at twenty-one) to highlight the deficiencies of the programme and the assumptions it carries. There is a precious moment of factual television as Apted embarks on yet another question about class, asking the women (again at twenty-eight) if they feel bitter about being working class in a society that 'probably gives one strata more opportunities than another'. The camera at this juncture pans along all three women, sitting side by side on a sofa and alights on Jackie smirking knowingly, as if she has been waiting for this to crop up. Her response is witty and telling:

> I don't think we honestly think about it until this programme comes up every seven years. I really don't think we ever think about it. I do not sit there thinking 'Oh, he was born into money, he's had more opportunities', it does not even cross my mind.

The 'three girls'' detachment from the programme and from Apted – that they question him and answer back, look resentfully towards him or refuse (particularly in Lynn's case) to answer questions they do not feel to be appropriate – is arguably also related to their gender. Simone de Beauvoir, John Berger and countless people since have noted that women are constructed, aware from an early age that they are being looked at, offering a performance of themselves to a masculine world that expects them to invite such looks and to abide by a fixed image of who and what they should be. The stereotypes of femininity are present in the lives of Sue, Jackie and Lynn in subliminal ways as well as in the series' compartmentalisation of them, for instance when Sue comments, at twenty-eight, 'The moment you get married, you're no longer yourself', adding after a moment's hesitation that 'that's how it should be'. Later, after her marriage has broken down and she has spent several years on her own, Sue says (in 42 Up) about being a single parent: 'I do the best I can.' This notion of doing what one can when the 'social script' one has been dealt fails to turn out as it should is a definitive one for many women. In fact, one of the interviewees for

Marilyn Gaunt's *Seven Up*-esque *Class of '62 – Still Going Strong* utters the exact same sentiment as Sue upon being asked how she copes looking after a mother in the early stages of dementia. In a similar manner Jackie refuses to let her severe and debilitating rheumatoid arthritis govern her life, closing her interview for *42 Up* – after Apted has mused (after reminiscing about Jackie at twenty-one) – that 'there was so much hope then':

> There still is, oh there still is. Don't make that mistake, Mike, I am down and I'm depressed about my illness but I'm certainly not down and depressed about my life. I'm lucky.

There is a pervasive sense that *Seven Up* never quite gives us the three East End women as they are, especially Jackie and Lynn. It is essentially a very middle-class series, packed with middle-class assumptions and neuroses about money and social standing, and so much of it is determined by the notion of each contributor's 'social script'. So much of the time Jackie and Lynn's responses defy and undermine this. Jackie (again), at twenty-eight, argues with Apted as he asks her if she is 'not missing out on what they have, their stake in the future' by not having children, replying with palpable resentment 'That's a terrible way to put it, you know.' Then Lynn espouses some what could be termed middle-class values about education and learning, but her life has never been changed by these: she went to grammar school, for instance, and has, since then, been a children's librarian in Tower Hamlets. How Lynn expresses her fulfilment in her job is quoted every seven years: 'Teaching children the beauty of books, watching their faces as books unfold to them is just fantastic.' To Lynn, however, books and a career have not functioned as the passport with which to 'escape her class', although they have been the path to personal fulfilment. Bruce talked about how Apted has mellowed over the years and his greater discernment about how individuals may or may not abide by their 'social script' emerges at the end of his interview with Lynn for *49 Up*. It is fair to acknowledge that Apted has always admired Lynn, even if she has not always been

113

welcoming or responsive to his probings. At the end of her segment of
49 Apted asks about her job 'It's been a hell of a commitment for you.
Has it been worth it all?'. Lynn answers 'Yes, it's been worth it – and
you better cut it, otherwise I'm going to cry', and gets up. It is in such
moments, which seem more pronounced when they occur – as they do
frequently – in the rather prickly exchanges between Apted and Jackie
or Lynn, that the complexity of the negotiations between the 'children'
and Apted, between what the 'children' want to say, what they feel
compelled to say and what they do not want to say emerges. The jostling
and detachment that characterise Apted's relationship to the 'girls'
serves as an apt metaphor for the series: the questioning of any
documentary subject can only ever tell you so much; it is especially in
these exchanges that the importance of the space between the notes, or
what remains unsaid, becomes as important as the notes sounded.

Conclusion

This book has been about both *Seven Up* and the historical impact of
Seven Up. When I asked Michael Apted to define the series' importance,
he gave me this answer:

> Its importance is in a way what it's become. It's become the longest
> documentary film to map out people's lives or celebrate them. So that's
> its importance – the fact that this document exists and is so far ahead of
> any of its copyists. I think that's enough. I'm not going to sit here and say
> it's changed people's lives. The achievement is having been carrying this
> project around for forty-two years. Not just my achievement but the
> people's in its achievement and the financiers' achievement – Granada
> have been there every seven years for forty-odd years. That's what it's about.
> Look no further than that. (Apted, 2007)

When Claire Lewis likewise contemplated the significance of *Seven Up*,
she put it like this:

> It's absolutely the most important thing I've ever done and will do and want
> to do, and it's held together by those relationships (between herself, Apted
> and the 'children'). There are no contracts on earth that could tie these
> people together; most of them don't want to do it – they have a loyalty to
> Michael and they have a loyalty to me and they also have a loyalty to the
> project because they understand, most of them, that it's unique and it's
> important. (Lewis, 2006)

And finally, this is what Nick and Bruce had to say about how they see *Seven Up* and why they stay involved:

> BRUCE: For myself it's not been a problem. First, they've been very kind to me by and large and, second, I know Michael and Claire and the cameraman quite well so I'm pleased to see them. I can imagine that for some of the others it's been an intrusion. They might in some ways feel a bit of a compulsion to carry on in that it is a sort of long document and if you decide you don't want to take part any more, you're abandoning something which has got a little bit of history to it and it's more difficult to break away from that. (Balden, 2006)

> NICK: You asked me if I'm happy to be in it. It's agonising to be in it, but it seems valuable. That's where I am on it. The fact that I'm traumatised to be in it is small potatoes compared to the fact that it's an important project. (Hitchon, 2006)

116 There is a discernible homogeneity to these statements: the notion that *Seven Up* is a significant *document* – both within the annals of television and documentary history and as a record of social and political history – and that it carries huge personal significance for those involved; to which I would add that the series has also been hugely important for those who have watched it all these years. As a text to watch and study, *Seven Up*'s richness lies in its detail: the cumulative effect of these lives having been lived in front of us over so many years.

When I embarked on this project I recall making grandiose claims for the series' importance as a social record of Britain. This is only in the very narrowest sense the case, for although it does offer a social history of sorts, it is necessarily patchy and inevitably tied to the perspectives and lives of those who have featured. *Seven Up*'s importance seems now to be far more primal than this: it has celebrated and valued the ordinary life. It clearly has neither proved nor disproved the conceit 'Give me a child until he is seven and I will give you the man' because lives as lived rather than theorised are predictable in some ways

Jackie, Lynn and Sue on the slide at the end of 'Seven Up!'   117

and unpredictable in others. Each instalment of *Seven Up!* now concludes with the final playground sequence from the original *World in Action*, Douglas Keay announcing the end of 'their very special day in London', when the children were invited to do 'just what they liked'. Keay then repeats the Jesuit maxim before closing with 'This has been a glimpse of Britain's future' over the final image of girls leaning back and swinging from a rope, their hair brushing the ground. Each time, as Keay's avuncular, patronising voice alights on each child in turn ('This is Nicholas ...', 'There's Tony') Apted inserts a contemporary image of each of them. 'Seven Up!' might not ultimately have delivered a glimpse into Britain's future, but the subsequent series has given an unmatched glimpse into its collective past.

Notes

1 Apted directed the Bond movie *The World Is Not Enough* (1999).

2 See Chapter 2 for a more detailed discussion of the impact of lightweight 16mm cameras and sound equipment on the evolution of documentary.

3 Xavier was beatified by Paul V on 25 October 1619 and canonised by Gregory XV on 12 March 1622 at the same time as Ignatius Loyola.

4 Furneaux has always taken issue with the decision to make *Seven Up* into a long-running series and that it was only because he thought *21 Up* was definitely going to be the last programme that he agreed to appear in it (Lewis, 2006).

5 Cf. Hitchon (2006).

6 For a more detailed discussion of recent documentaries in relation to *Seven Up* see the next chapter.

7 BFI Pamphlet, 791.492: 942: Free Cinema: Programme Notes for the Seasons of Free Cinema held at the National Film Theatre during 1956–9.

8 For this interpretation of realism in early 1960s television and film in Britain I am indebted to Robert Murphy.

9 For a more expansive discussion of this idea see Bruzzi (2006), particularly the Introduction and Chapter 6.

10 Cf. also my discussion of the journey structure in documentary in *New Documentary* (2nd edition, 2006).

11 BBC press office, 6 May 2004, press release on <bbc.co.uk>.

12 Channel 4, 5 April 1985, 21.30–22.15.

13 Cf. Brian Winston (1995).

14 Cf. Bruzzi (2000), Chapter 2, for my discussion of the uses of voiceover in documentary.

15 Twenty children were selected to feature in this original programme. If Michelle is not familiar now to viewers, it is because she evidently was one of the six who, after Apted had been asked to make *7 Plus Seven*, was not chosen to feature in the follow-up film.

16 Neil never reveals, despite persistent questioning from Apted, what his 'nervous complaint' is. He acknowledges each time that he is unwell or has been unwell, that he has sought medical help etc., but he goes no further than this.

17 Bruce and Penny's wedding was one of the rare times when Apted and the crew filmed an event before the seven years had come around.

18 Cf. also my discussion of the journey structure in documentary in Bruzzi (2006).

19 Nick Hitchon takes exception to the way in which he feels Apted stresses, in his voiceover, that he went to 'the *local* grammar school', indicating that he was not 'impressed by that' (Hitchon, 2006).

20 Cf., for instance, *21 Up* as Apted, towards the beginning of the film, says to Nick 'I suppose of all the seven-year-olds, the original ones, you're the big success story.' Nick's response is not to accept this and to counter that he has not done anything special or 'out of the ordinary'.

21 Clearly, this must have derived in part from the fact that of the three only Andrew has been involved all the way through the series.

22 An exception to this is Apted's treatment of Charles Furneaux, from *28 Up*, the point at which he stopped taking part. As Charles became a documentary film-maker, producer and commissioning editor, Apted has always felt his desertion of the series particularly keenly. In *28 Up*, for example, Apted says of Charles's decision to stop taking part: 'Charles has found a career suited to his talents. At the BBC he makes documentary films. He decided *not* to take part in *this* film'. In interview he added:

'I could never understand ... how someone who earns his living doing this job won't be part of it. If you live by the sword you die by the sword' (Apted, 2007).

23 Cf. Episode 2, *The Trap* (Adam Curtis, BBC2, 18 March 2007).

24 Cf. Chapter 1 for a brief discussion of documentaries that follow the same structure as *Seven Up*, but that only follow the lives of women.

Bibliography

Apted, Michael, Interview with the author, 4 January 2006.

Apted, Michael, Interview with the author, 5 March 2007.

Balden, Bruce, Interview with the author, 23 November 2006.

Banks Smith, Nancy, '*Seven Plus Seven*' (review), *Guardian*, 16 December 1970.

Banks Smith, Nancy, '*Twenty-One*' (review), *Guardian*, 10 May 1977.

Barker, Nicholas, Interview with the author for *New Documentary: A Critical Introduction*, 10 September 1999.

Barnes, Julian, 'The Granada Fourteen', *The Observer*, 25 November 1984.

Bond, Matthew, 'Their Story So Far ...', *Daily Telegraph*, 23 July 1998: 40.

Britton, Andrew, 'Their Finest Hour: Humphrey Jennings and the British Imperial Myth of World War II', *CineAction!* vol. 18, 1989: 37–44.

Bruzzi, Stella, *New Documentary: A Critical Introduction* (London: Routledge, 2000).

Bruzzi, Stella, *New Documentary* (2nd edn) (London: Routledge, 2006).

Butler, Judith, *Gender Trouble: Feminism and the Subversion of Identity* (London and New York: Routledge, 1990).

Davies, Jessica, 'My Life Began the Day My Marriage Ended', *Daily Mail*, 20 May 1991: 13.

Day-Lewis, Sean, 'Properties of Bores Nicely Contrasted', *Daily Telegraph*, 10 May 1977.

Durgnat, Raymond, *A Mirror for England: British Movies from Austerity to Affluence* (London: Faber and Faber, 1970).

Goddard, Peter, Corner, John and Richardson, Kay, *Public Issue Television: World in Action 1963–98* (Manchester: Manchester University Press, 2007)

Goddard, Peter, Corner, John and Richardson, Kay (2001) 'The Formation of *World in Action*: A Case Study in the History of Current Affairs Journalism', *Journalism* vol. 2 no. 1, pp. 73–90.

Granada Television, Press release for *7 Plus Seven*, 1970.

Grove, Valerie, 'The Boy and the Man and the Good Woman', *Evening Standard*, 23 November 1984: 25.

Hamilton, Ian, '*Twenty-One*' (review), *New Statesman*, 13 May 1977.

Hitchon, Nick, Interview with the author, 21 December 2006.

Hoggart, Richard, *The Uses of Literacy* (Harmondsworth: Penguin, 1957 [1965]).

ITA paper 126, 'A Review of Network Current Affairs Programmes (January–June 1964), Memorandum by Mr Sendall, 2 September 1964.

Jeffries, Stuart, 'Get Real', *Guardian*, 6 July 2006.

Lewis, Claire, Interview with the author, 13 September 2006.

Lewis, Claire and Davis, Kelly, *35 Up* (London: Network Books, 1991).

Low, Robert, Untitled item on *28 Up*, *The Observer*, 2 December 1984: 3.

Moran, Joe, 'Childhood, Class and Memory in the *Seven Up!* Films', *Screen* vol. 43 no. 4, Winter 2002: 387–402.

Nahra, Carol, 'Michael Apted and *42 Up*', *International Documentary* vol. 18 nos 1–2, January–February 1999: 22–3.

National Film Theatre, Roundtable discussion on Free Cinema with Kevin Macdonald, Walter Lasselly, Lorenza Mazzetti, Karel Reisz, 22 March 2001 <www.bfi.org.uk>.

Neale, Steve, 'Melodrama and Tears,' *Screen* vol. 27 no. 6, November–December 1986: 6–22.

Nichols, Bill, *Representing Reality: Issues and Concepts of Documentary* (Bloomington and Indianapolis: Indiana University Press, 1991).

Nichols, Bill, *Blurred Boundaries: Questions of Meaning in Contemporary Culture* (Bloomington and Indianapolis: Indiana University Press, 1994).

Paphides, Peter, '*28 Up*', *Time Out*, 15–22 July 1998: 26.

Purser, Philip, '*28 Up*', *Sunday Telegraph* (review), 25 November 1984: 17.

Sarris, Andrew, 'Notes on the Class Struggle', *Village Voice*, 22 October 1985: 51.

Schwabsky, Barry, 'The Eyes Have It: Gillian Wearing on Diane Arbus', *Artforum*, February 2004.

Tate, Webpage on Gillian Wearing, by Jemima Montagu <www.tate.org.uk>, March 2001.

White, Hayden, *The Content of the Form: Narrative, Discourse and Historical Representation* (Baltimore, MD and London: Johns Hopkins University Press, 1987).

Williamson, Harold, ' "Appear on the Box Again!" No, Thank You!', *The Listener*, 6 January 1983: 8.

Winston, Brian, *Claiming the Real: The Documentary Film Revisited* (London: BFI, 1995).

Credits

Seven Up

the participants
Jacqueline Bassett
Nicholas Hitchon
Neil Hughes
Tony Walker
John Brisby
Charles Furneaux
Andrew Brackfiield
Paul Kligerman
Simon Basterfiield
Bruce Balden
Suzanne Lusk
Lynn Johnson
Peter Davies
Susan Davis
and their families

'Seven Up!'

United Kingdom/1964

Granada presents

this edition prepared by
Paul Almond
with
Michael Apted

uncredited
researcher
Gordon McDougall
photography
Michael Boultbee
David Samuelson
commentator
Douglas Keay

first shown as part of series
***World in Action* on ITV on 5**
May 1964 (22.05–23.00)

7 Plus Seven

United Kingdom/1970

Granada Television
International

directed by
Michael Apted
produced by
Michael Apted
cameraman
Tony Mander
film editor
David Naden
research
Margaret Bottomley
sound
Neil Kingsbury
Peter Walker

© Granada International
Productions Limited

first shown on ITV on 15
December 1970
(21.00–22.00)

Twenty-One

United Kingdom/1977

Granada Television
International

production
Michael Apted
Margaret Bottomley
camera
George Jesse Turner
editing
Andrew Page
sound
Alan Bale
dubbing
John Whitworth

© Granada International
Productions Limited

first shown as part of series
***World in Action* on ITV on 9**
May 1977 (21.00–22.00,
22.30–23.30)

28 Up

United Kingdom/1984

Granada

directed by
Michael Apted
produced by
Michael Apted
executive producer
Steve Morrison
camera
George Jesse Turner
editors
Oral Norrie Ottey
Kim Horton
2nd editing director
Eva Kolouchova
sound
Nick Steer
dubbing
John Whitworth
research
Claire Lewis
programme consultant
Margaret Bottomley
production assistant
Jacki Harding
graphic designer
Keith Aldred

©Granada UK

part I: first shown on ITV on
20 November 1984
(22.30–23.40)
part II: first shown on ITV on
21 November 1984
(22.35–00.05)

35 Up

United Kingdom/1991

a Granada production for ITV

directed by
Michael Apted
produced by
Michael Apted

executive producer
Rod Caird
series editor
Claire Lewis
photography
George Jesse Turner
additional photography
Howard Somers
film editor
Kim Horton
sound
Nick Steer
additional sound
Harry Brookes
Chris Atkinson
stills photography
Ged Murray
dubbing mixer
Tony Anscombe
dubbing editor
Mark Senior
graphics
Phil Buckley
electrician
Graham Mitchell
programme manager
Gayle Broughall
programme accountant
David Buckley
production assistant
Jacki Turner
assistant to Michael Apted
Ann Pollack
programme associates
Paul Almond (7 Up)
Gordon McDougall (7 Up)
Margaret Bottomley (21 Up)

© Granada Television

first shown as part of series
World in Action on ITV on 22
May 1991 (20.00–22.15)

42 Up

United Kingdom/1998

a Granada production for BBC

directed by
Michael Apted
produced by
Michael Apted
executive producers
Stephen Lambert (for BBC)

Ruth Pitt (for Granada
Television)
co-producer
Claire Lewis
photography
George Jesse Turner
film editor
Kim Horton
sound
Nick Steer
assistant camera
Michael Costello
electrician
Stuart Wilson
dubbing
John Whitworth
dubbing editors
John Crumpton
John Rutherford
Paul Horsfall
graphic designer
Phil Buckley
production co-ordinators
Jacki Turner
Jackie McKinney
Jeanney Kim
programme associates
Paul Almond (7 Up)
Gordon McDougall (7 Up)
Margaret Bottomley (21 Up)
researcher
Melanie Archer

© Granada Television

part I: first shown on BBC1 on
21 July 1998 (21.30–22.35)
part II: first shown on BBC1 on
22 July 1998 (21.30–22.45)
Granada's original *World in
Action* series title card shown
at the start of both BBC1
transmissions.

49 Up

United Kingdom/2005

directed by
Michael Apted
produced by
Claire Lewis
Michael Apted
executive producer
Bill Jones

photography
George Jesse Turner
sound
Nick Steer
film editor
Kim Horton
camera assistants
Jason Trench
Matt Gathercole
Australia Team [part I]
Kathryn Millis
Leo Sullivan
Emma Gillam
Bulgaria Team [part II]
Jemma Jupp
Owen Scurfiield
Nic Jones
on-line editor
Ian Brown
colourist
Neil Parker
graphic designer
Susan Bodicoat
dubbing mixers
Dion Stuart
Samantha Handy
production co-ordinators
Helen Breslin
Jacki Turner
Cort Kristensen
production manager
Karen Stockton

7 Up directed by
Paul Almond
7 Up researched by
Michael Apted
Gordon McDougall

"In memory of Tim Hewat,
Founder/Producer of *World in
Action* who inspired 7 Up"

© Granada Television Ltd

part I: first shown as part of
series *World in Action* on ITV1
on 15 September 2005
(21.00–22.30)
part II: first shown as part of
series *World in Action* on ITV1
on 22 September 2005
(21.00–22.30)

123

Index